LIVING THE FIVE WEALTH PRINCIPLES™

C. Anthony Harris

Living The Five Wealth Principles™

Copyright © 2006 by C. Anthony Harris.

Published by LifeWorks Publications, Ltd.

ISBN: 978-0-9791207-2-5

For information write:
LifeWorks Publications, Ltd.
10620 Southern Highlands Parkway,
Las Vegas, NV 89141
702.577.2880 or FAX: 702.922.1810
Visit our website at www.vizionone.com

If you purchased this book without a cover you should be aware that this book is stolen property. It was reported as "unsold and destroyed" to the publisher, and neither the author nor the publisher has received any payment for this "stripped book."

All Rights reserved.
No part of this book may be reproduced in any form or by any electronic or mechanical means including information storage and retrieval systems without permission in writing from the publisher, except by a reviewer, who may quote brief passages in a review.

Foreword

It is an esteemed honor to have been chosen to endorse Living The Five Wealth Principles. This book is an extraordinary work and an enjoyable guide to a way of life that leads to success.

As a sociologist, educator, writer and community leader, I review lots of information designed to empower others. Living The Five Wealth Principles is among the most positive and most refreshing works I have ever read.

This book will motivate you to continue building upon your foundations of success and will inspire you to encourage others to do the same. Living The Five Wealth Principles will add value and direction to your life. It will prepare you to pursue that which you deserve. Read it. Enjoy it. Live it.

Peace and Blessings,

Odida T. Quamina
Justice of the Peace
Toronto, Canada

I dedicate my first book to everyone who has had an influence in my life, my development and my success.

Specifically, to Herbert Harris (Herbs), my father, for showing me how to be a man, accept responsibility and understand the importance of providing for your family; my grandparents Doris, Pearl and Cyril who demanded that I learn, live and come to like **discipline**; my sisters Sharon and Terriann who make my job as an older brother both interesting and exciting; my mother, Shirley, my anchor for her loving prayers and encouragement in support of my desire to become a successful entrepreneur - I could have never gotten this far without you; my protégé, Cory Anthony Harris for being a patient son - my confidence, strength and power are drawn from your existence; to my God sent Angel and the most wonderful woman in the world, Donna Maria Thompson for embracing my vision and paving the way to all possibilities - you are truly Living The Five Wealth Principles; and finally, to all of you who are reading this book. I dedicate this book in honor of your support in helping me to create a movement of positive, powerful and successful people all over the world who will enjoy wealth and success-spiritually, mentally, physically, professionally and financially through Living The Five Wealth Principles.

"To God be the glory for the things He has done!"

~ C. Anthony Harris

Acknowledgements

Living The Five Wealth Principles has been embedded in my thoughts, actions and way of life for years. It has afforded me success and changed my life tremendously. Through living these principles I have been truly blessed and it is an honor and a privilege to share my success with you.

My sincere thanks and praises go to the Universe who has cleverly guided me on my journey. The Universe has blessed me with the wisdom to figure out what it takes to become and to remain successful. Through Divine Intervention, grace and guidance, I have fulfilled one of my lifelong dreams. Thanks be to You for all you have done! I thank everyone who had a hand in this publication.

Sincere gratitude goes to Dr. Michael Beckwith, my spiritual advisor for teaching me how to move through life with confidence, strength, power and ease. To those who have traveled with me on my journey- thank you, thank you, thank you. Your love and support is and always will be priceless.

Dr. Odida Quamina
Vito Terracciano
Cedric Rashad
Jonathan Aluko
Barry Donalson
Ruben Gonzales
Wade Woodrow Woodson
Nick Pile
Wendell Strozier

Table of Contents

PREFACE — 11

INTRODUCTION — 19

Success…It Is What It Is-Or Is It? — 26
The Transformation — 38
A True Mentor — 46

PERSISTENCY — 49

Outside of the Norm — 52
Persistency and You — 67
Strategies for Success — 75

CONSISTENCY — 85

Consistency and You — 90
No…Stop…Don't — 97
Strategies for Success — 131

DISCIPLINE   137

    The Difficulty
With Discipline   144
Discipline and You   151
Conquering Your Fear   172
Strategies for Success   187

URGENCY   193

    Create Your Circumstance   199
Urgency and You   201
Strategies for Success   209

EXCITEMENT   213

    Excitement and You   217
Rome Wasn't
Built In A Day   218
Strategies for Success   223

CONCLUSION   227

Appendix 231

Table I
    If I…Then What   233

LFWP LifePlan
For Success Journal   235

Preface

Every one of us at some point or another has boggled our mind with questions about our purpose in life. You know, the type of questions you have difficulty admitting that you don't know the answers to and have no clue about where to find them.

I have often wondered and asked myself- Why am I here, what should I be doing, why am I not fulfilled, what is it that I am doing wrong, why am I not as successful as I strive to be and what do I need to do to get better? After some very intense soul searching, I thought I had the answers, but to my surprise, I still did not have a clue.

I thought that when I "arrived" at success, I would immediately be fulfilled. In order to become successful, all I had to do was work hard. If I wanted more success, I simply would have to work harder; so, I did just that. I worked hard!

I pushed myself to unimaginable limits, perfected my craft on my job, bought every self-help book that interested me, read everything I could get my hands on and even discussed my dreams and aspirations with my family and friends.

I memorized entire sections of *Think and Grow Rich* (Napoleon Hill), internalized the *21 Irrefutable Laws of Leadership* (Dr. John C. Maxwell) and even developed my life's plan to go from *Good to Great (*Jim Collins). You name it, I did it, but I never got any closer to the success I dreamed about for my life. What was the problem?

I was persistent, I was focused, I knew what I wanted, I was willing to work for it and I wasn't afraid of hard work. I could not understand why I could not get a grip on the dreams and intentions I had for my life. I knew that I had what it took in me but could not quite figure how to get it out. What was I doing wrong?

Funny thing is I was not doing anything "wrong". I was simply using my efforts and expending my energies on the wrong stuff. I wanted success, but had taken no time to define what "success" actually meant to me or how I would personally achieve it. Through reading how-to-books and the stories of others, I was increasing my appetite for and knowledge of what success should be, but I was not doing anything concrete to achieve the success I desired. I was simply trying to swim upstream without getting wet. Without a clear definition of success, it was impossible to map out a plan for achieving it.

Realizing that knowledge without practice was unproductive, I developed a new way of living. I did more, desired less and began to experience the success I had often dreamed about in the past.

In my "defining moment", I made a decision to take what I wanted from life, refused to settle for what it was giving and didn't give up until I got it. I *N-E-V-E-R* GAVE UP!

In fact, through my determination I became very successful in all aspects of my life- the spiritual, mental, physical, professional, and financial. However, as I accomplished more of my goals and began to experience more success, I again found myself wondering. How did I go from *wanting, to having, to keeping, to increasing* the success I now enjoy? More importantly, how do I help others to do the same?

I went back to the drawing board and this time focused more on the things I was doing right. Five years later, I found my answers and they are all in this book.

You see, through consistent self-reflection, growing pains, hard work and determination, I discovered that I achieve, maintain and increase success through *Living* The Five Wealth Principles... Persistency, Consistency, Discipline, Urgency and Excitement™. I also discovered I am not alone. Many people have or have had problems achieving and maintaining the levels of success they desire and are still searching for a solution.

Living The Five Wealth Principles™ has the answer- a way of life that works. The bottom line is this; "Life Works When You Work It™ Through the practice of these principles I have learned to put things into perspective and work life; to move from all talk and no action to all action. The daily practice of these principles has added a tremendous amount of joy, peace, strength, power and confidence to my life and it will do the same for you. But, like anything else- we have to use it, or we'll lose it.

It really is simple. In order to become and remain successful you and I must maintain a level of Persistency, Consistency, Discipline, Urgency and Excitement that is above what has been "normal" for us in the past. We must learn, internalize, and practice Living the Five Wealth Principles™ daily and be determined never to give in to negativity or give up on ourselves. I guarantee, when we commit to doing this; we commit to achieving success.

The principles, ideas, strategies and information I share with you in this book are not just empty thoughts. These principles, if put into action, will change your life. I know, they changed mine and I embrace with excitement and great enthusiasm the opportunity to use my knowledge and experiences to help you change yours.

Congratulations on taking the first step toward the brightest, most rewarding, and most successful life ever. Share this book and your experience with everyone you meet and together, let's create a movement of successful, positive, powerful and productive leaders who are Living The Five Wealth Principles™, enjoying wealth- spiritually, mentally, physically, professionally, financially and changing the quality of life all over the world.

Come, join me on the LFWP life plan to success and let's win!

~ C. Anthony Harris

A man is great not because he has not failed.
A man is great because failure has not stopped him.

~ CONFUCIOUS

===============

INTRODUCTION

Work towards that one bright day when the sun rises over your mountaintop.
~*Adaptation Ziggy Marley*

Success ~ If you jump into the fire you will get burned; if you jump into the water you will get wet; if you jump into despair you will be destroyed, but if you jump into success you will - get my point?

~ C. Anthony Harris

Success. Who is it? What is it? When will I get it? Where will I find it? Why do I need it? And most importantly, how do I achieve it? The answers to these questions have puzzled us all at some time or another. You hunger for success, but what, *really*, is success?

According to technical definition, success is defined as favorable or desired outcomes and/or the gaining of wealth and fame. In accordance with my experience, I dare to define success as a set of personally desired outcomes relative to personal goals and ambitions carefully thought out and defined by *you.*

To begin your journey to the life you have always wanted, you must determine what success means to you in very real and certain terms before you begin working at making it happen.

Do you simply want to attain a favorable outcome from the things you do in life or do you want the wealth and/or fame that could come along with your efforts?

I urge you to answer these questions honestly and prepare to put into action the fundamental principles outlined in this book that will change the way you live. **Persistency, Consistency, Discipline, Urgency and Excitement** are the five wealth principles that you must learn, internalize, and practice everyday in order to attain the dimensions of success you desire.

While success is a very abstract concept, it becomes very concrete when applied to our individual lives. Success, for example, with the high school student may be to graduate from his or her program with honors. For the failing "at-risk" student, success may be just to graduate, even if it means they are the last ranking member of their class. For some it may be to simply survive another day. For the stay-at-home mother of three, success might be to raise her children before embarking upon any other endeavors. The college graduate might define success as landing the perfect position in "Corporate America", getting married, parenting 2.5 children, building a home in the suburbs and driving the latest change over Lexus at 12:01 am the day of its release. For others, it may be entrepreneurship, wealth, or fame. Whatever the circumstance, true success, can only be defined by YOU.

    Contrary to popular belief, success is not defined by how much money you make, what car you drive, where you live, what church or organization you belong to, or any of the other "industry standards" we often use as measuring sticks. Again, true success is defined by you.

> **To guess is cheap, to guess wrong is expensive.**
>
> ~ Author unknown

YOU decide what your favorable or desired outcome is for your life. What is it that would make you happy; keep you excited; make you stay focused on the positives of life, and ultimately take care of your needs and appease your wants? What is it that you will work at with persistence, on a consistent basis, with the necessary discipline, coupled with a sense of urgency and excitement? *What does success mean to you?*

If you don't know, quickly, find out. You cannot and you will not find the success you desire if you don't know what you are looking for. Trust me. Success does actually exist and it exists in abundance. You can have as much or as little of it as you want but you have to know *what* you want before you can decide how much of it you want. I strongly urge you to take the time to define the meaning of success in your life. If you don't you will find yourself in one or more of the following situations.

1. If you do not take the time to define what success means to you, you will always find yourself trying to meet the expectations of others; expectations that may be too high or too low or those that may not even be aligned with what you really want.

2. If you don't take the time to define what success means for you and your life, you will always feel as though you are swimming upstream without a paddle. You will have no direction, no goal to which you work towards and nothing you can look back on to say "Wow, I did it".

3. If you do not take the time to think about your personal definition of success, you have wasted both time and money. You will never bring any vision you have to completion and you will always be looking for that "something" that will satisfy you. All of your self-development investments will be a waste of both time and money.

Maximize Your Investment

Living The Five Wealth Principles is a roadmap to success. It is an investment that will do nothing for you if you are only reading it for enjoyment. You have to read it with the sincere intention of practicing each and every one of the principles outlined and applying them to a definitive vision of the success you seek. These principles cannot be applied to thin air. You have to know what success means to you and begin the application and practice of these principles daily. These principles must be so ingrained into your daily routine that Living the Five Wealth Principles becomes a way of life for you and not just another book you started reading and did not finish. Maximize your investment!

Success…It Is What It Is, Or Is It?

As a young adult my best friend from high school Stephen Walcott and I often fantasized about becoming successful entrepreneurs, owning multimillion dollar businesses and living life to the fullest. We even tried a few ventures here and there in the area of entrepreneurship and were good at it, so we thought. We promoted parties, sold cassettes, raffled off the neighbor's dog on occasion and better yet, sold that geeky pair of sneakers Mom bought with her hard earned money for pennies on the dollar, covering our tracks by telling her someone stole them during gym class. We had big dreams, small projects, but big dreams, nevertheless.

Stephen and I worked hard and appeared to be very good at what we were trying to do. We sat down, mapped out our plans and made things happen. Whenever we had a project we thought was successful, we would dream about our future. We'd convince ourselves there was nothing we couldn't do. We were going to be wealthy and live life to the fullest. The problem was, when it was all said and done, all we had done was *TALK*. We never achieved the success about которой we dreamed. What had we done wrong? I'll tell you.

In our detailed descriptions of success and the intricate plans we had for our lives, neither Stephen nor I ever really defined "success" relative to our personal goals and ambitions. We simply adopted and settled for the most popular myth-money, cars and women. We both had the desire, the drive and the dreams to become millionaires, but we did not give any attention to what it would take to get us there in reality.

We never sought out mentors to teach us what we needed to know. Neither

Stephen nor I ever did any research on who, what, when, where or how millionaires came into their existence. I don't even think we could have named three millionaires we would try to mimic. Of course, we knew success was synonymous with hard work, perseverance, patience, and discipline. But, what we did not know was that, in order to really taste the fruits of success, we had to define it before attempting to achieve it. We had to begin putting the horse before the *buggy* if we wanted to move forward.

Show Me The Money

To make money Stephen and I often threw parties. We would rent out a reception hall, invite everyone we knew and party until the sun came up. We thought, if we threw a party, invited 100 people and 95 showed up, we were successful. It wasn't until we counted the cash at the end of the night that we discovered 65 of the 95 who showed up were our friends or family and we'd let them in free. Only then did we make the miraculous discovery that we were not so successful after all.

You see, in the beginning, we defined success by the number of people in attendance. The party was packed, the music was right and everyone was having a good time. I mean this party was the bomb! In the end, however, when our focus changed from a good time to calculating the money we thought we'd made to cover expenses, we were in for a rude awakening.

By good time standards, we were extremely successful promoters; but, when the time came to pay bills, our good time, instantaneously became an example of bad business. Had we, in the beginning, defined success by monetary standards, our focus and our outcome would have been totally different. In other words, if our parents had showed up at the party, they would have had to pay.

The point is that it is extremely imperative that you carefully define success before you begin your journey towards achieving it. Otherwise, you will find yourself chasing after your dreams for the rest of your life and will never see them come true.

Without a true definition of the success you seek, you will never become focused enough to apply the principles of wealth to your life nor will you experience any of the benefits produced by your self-help investments. Only when you have turned the abstract cloud of "success" into a concrete cornerstone can you begin to build your foundation. At that moment you are ready to begin Living The Five Wealth Principles and can begin the process of turning your life around for the better.

Your new moon in life can't come until your old one has gone ~ author unknown

Don't be alarmed if you don't quite know what success is for you at this exact moment. I myself have had to do a lot of soul searching and have come to realize that success is relative.

In 1996, I had the idea that I was *successful*. I had a good job working as a Systems Analyst with the Federal Government, was making a nice salary and was content with going to work and doing my best. Working on the job for 12 years, I knew my craft well. I was stable, I had benefits and I knew exactly what day and time my direct deposit would be in my account and the second the "funds (would be) available". Depending on the time of the month, I knew exactly how much free money I could blow off on those much anticipated weekend splurges. I was, in the eyes of my parents, my son and all of the hard working 9 to 5'ers, *successful*. All of that changed, however, seemingly in the twinkling of an eye.

The Lottery

One afternoon, Stephen, my dream sharer, if you will, came to see me. He was so excited, I thought he had won the lottery or something and was coming to tell me that our dream of becoming millionaires had finally seen the light of day. Well, he didn't hit the lottery, literally. But, he had heard about some twenty-five year old kid who had become a millionaire after involving himself with long distance phone services and Stephen convinced me to attend a Saturday seminar at the Sheraton in Manhattan, NYC. I remember it like it was yesterday.

The hotel was filled with extremely positive energy. In all of my days, I had never experienced so much positive feedback in one place. There were approximately 500 people in the room anxiously waiting, curiously anticipating this 25 year old, African-American millionaire's thoughts on success.

After a few minutes, this "kid" is greeted with a roar of excitement from the audience. He comes out dancing and smiling so wide he could have eaten a banana sideways. He was polished from head to toe. He was positive, smooth, happy and at peace. This guy was synonymous with success.

I was fortunate to have had a front row seat and prepared my mind to soak in every tidbit of information made available. I was curious, excited, and fully understood what a valuable opportunity laid before me. I was getting first hand information, straight from the proverbial horse's mouth and I was mesmerized. Wow!

Following a spectacular, mind-gripping presentation, I had the pleasure of meeting this young man personally and let me tell you, that five minutes was the most impacting, life changing experience I have ever encountered. I have heard before that people's spirits are transferable but to have the experience is something amazing.

The Lightning Bolt

When the gentleman shook my hand, I could feel his power. He shook my hand with a firm grip, looked me straight in the eye and promoted a sense of strength, confidence, and positive power that seemed to have struck me like lightening. I could not believe this guy was only 25 years old. He had it all at such a young age-wealth, personality, wisdom, charisma. It seemed as if my grandfather for whom I have the utmost respect had instantaneously appeared in the edifice of this 25-year-old kid.

He went on to ask me some questions and told me that he could see my greatness. He told me that he could see himself in me and expressed how happy he was that I had come out to investigate the opportunity. Now, at the time, I was not a millionaire, but I sure felt like one. No one had ever told me that before. No one had ever made me feel as though they believed in me the way this guy did.

He asked me, "Do you see an opportunity for yourself?" And that's when I began to figure this thing out.

In order to become successful, I had to see what he saw in me! I had to see not only my potential for greatness but the benefits of the opportunities that were being presented. I had to see my success, at the time, in direct selling and I had to go after it.

Well, I replied, nervously, "Yes, I do see an opportunity".

He immediately asked when I planned on getting started. I responded by saying that I was not sure. He, of course, dug a little deeper and presented this question to me "If you see something for yourself that will change your life and the lives your family, why are you not sure? Why won't you get started?"

Embarrassingly, I explained that I didn't have the money and was not sure when I would get it. Now, this is where that 100 watt light bulb in my head was turned on and my thoughts of success went from the dullness of dim to the miraculous, marvelous light.

The gentleman asked, "Carl, what do you do for a living?"

I stuck my chest out and confidently responded, "I am a Systems Analyst with the Federal Government". After all that was my success story and I was proud of it.

He said, "Great, how long have you been doing this?"

I replied even more proudly, "12 years."

He placed his hands on my shoulder and came closer to me, looked me straight in the eyes and said,

"Great, a Systems Analyst. Well, I am an electrical engineer, so we have *some* things in common. You've been doing this for 12 years and you don't have $500 dollars to invest in changing your financial future?"

I was so embarrassed and felt so intimidated it seemed as if I was the only one in the room and the walls were closing in on me. The interesting thing about it all, however, was at no time did I feel inferior. He had only asked me a mind-blowing question that I should have had courage enough to ask myself.

As the conversation continued, I began to sense his genuine concern for my future. His heartfelt sincerity let me know, right then, that this was a man whose lead I could follow. He went on to solidify my discovery that a change was necessary when he said, "if after 12 years on a great job, you don't have $500 to invest in changing your life, Carl, do you think the next 12 years will be any different?"

I was absolutely speechless. It hit me like a ton of bricks. For the first time I realized, I was not as *successful* as I believed!

The moment was bitter sweet and my first instinct was to become defensive. How dare he? This guy just met me. He doesn't know me. He does not know how hard I work or what I sacrifice to put food in my son's mouth. The nerve! Here this guy is pretending to befriend me and show concern, and then he insults me. I thought, with friends like him who needs enemies?

Then, the voice of reason made me understand. This guy was only telling me the truth; the truth that I really was not as successful as I thought. I was successful according to everyone but my own standards.

In that defining moment, I discovered I had not taken the time to define what success really meant to me. This gentleman had only whacked me over the head with the stick of truth; the truth that revealed how I had simply been settling for what life was giving me instead of taking what I wanted; the truth that unless, I was willing to take the leap of faith that would change my circumstance, I would remain stagnant.

This 25 year-old kid made me realize the truth that I would always live in the shadows of success and never experience its light; that unless I got myself together, my dream of becoming a successful millionaire would always be just that, a dream.

With all of this going through my head, I felt bewildered. I was in a daze and everything seemed to be in a blur. Then, he spoke again. He said to me,

> "Carl, let me say this to you. You can take or leave it, but I am going to give you three foundations of wealth. Think about them and if you are serious about your life, meet me on Tuesday night at 7 pm at the Crown Plaza on Broadway. 1) Never work a job the rest of your life for money, 2) Copy successful people. 3) Make money while you sleep. "My friend," he said, "if you are serious, I'll see you on Tuesday, if not God bless, and good luck."

He then turned to meet and greet the next person in the line of 300 plus waiting patiently behind for the chance to meet him. I observed for about 30 minutes longer and witnessed, in astonishment, him giving the same love, concern and sense of empowerment he had given me to others.

I walked away feeling both great, and somewhat saddened. For the first time in my life I heard my inner voice telling me, "You got it Carl, and you can be just like that guy," but I did not know exactly how or where to begin. I didn't know if I could even really do it. Hell, I didn't have the $500 necessary to even think about getting started and no idea about where I could get it. I was excited about the opportunity, but felt defeated before I even entered the game.

> Never work a job for the rest of your life for money.
>
> Copy successful people.
>
> Make money while you sleep.

The Transformation

It took me two months to raise the money and I did everything. And I do mean everything, well, with the exception of selling dinners on the corner in front of the local community center. I saved, I worked extra hours, and I even tapped into my rainy day resources. While raising the money, however, I attended every presentation, every meeting, and every training session made available. I took notes, I listened, I asked questions and I learned. More importantly, I surrounded myself with positive, young, vibrant, successful leaders and took advantage of my new life-changing mentor.

Chance meetings with my mentor were always uncomfortable. I never wanted him to feel as though I was trying to take advantage of the situation. He would always ask if I had gotten started and my answer was always indefinite, "soon". Then, to my astonishment, my mentor began to edify me. Me! I couldn't believe it.

I was sitting in the meeting, taking in as much information as I possibly could and making a strong effort to concentrate on the business. I engaged a mental warfare and became determined to block out my frustration with feeling as if I did not belong and stayed focused on being positive. To my surprise, I heard my name.

"And before we close I would like to commend you." "Carl, he told them, "has not allowed his lack of money to stop him from gaining a wealth of knowledge."

My mentor recognized my determination; my drive; my competitive spirit and my refusal to accept defeat before I had actually entered the game. I became his example of determination and he continued to encourage me.

He taught me to change my vocabulary; how not to confirm that I was broke, but to admit that I was temporarily, "financially challenged." I learned so much in those sixty days that my life went through a complete paradigm shift. I became more and more confident in my own abilities. I became more aware of my desires for my life and found myself growing in thought, ideology, and knowledge at an alarming pace. I began to build upon my mentor's foundations for wealth and started the process of copying successful people.

The Change

It's really simple, in order to become successful, you have to first define success according to your goals and ambitions, seek out successful people, observe their thoughts and actions, and begin to mimic what you witness.

You have to change your thoughts, start thinking like a successful person and start making small changes in preparation for "the big change".

It's a well-known fact in nature that when life ends as a caterpillar, it begins as a beautiful butterfly. Think about it. That same squirmy caterpillar who in the beginning inches its way around in the dirt and grime of the earth develops into a beautiful butterfly free to fly to some of the most beautiful most exotic places on earth.

At one point in its life, the caterpillar is ignored, viewed as just another insect. After its metamorphosis, however, people spend thousands of dollars planting exotic "butterfly gardens" so as to attract its beauty. They become less concerned about what the caterpillar used to be and simply mesmerized by what it has become.

> When life ends as a caterpillar. It begins as a beautiful butterfly.

Find someone whose success you admire and begin your metamorphosis. Begin feeding your mind with positive, progressive thoughts and actions, understanding that success is 90% mental and 10% activity. We're all familiar with the phrase you are what you eat. Well, let me challenge you to internalize the truth you are what you think… "as a man thinketh in his heart, so he is" Proverbs 23:7.

Become less concerned about what you didn't do and more concerned as I did about what you are currently doing to change your life. Start small if you have to and remember that small changes added together equal larger ones.

It's just like money, every penny counts. You can't technically call yourself a millionaire if you've only earned $999,999.99. You're a penny short. Now, some of you may say, well it's only a penny and you're right, but it's the penny that makes the difference between your status as the potential millionaire and the actual millionaire. It's just like life; it is what it is so don't short-change yourself and accept anything less than success. Every change you make counts!

From Thinking To Knowing…

I started my change by programming my mind to think that I could be as successful as the people with whom I had surrounded myself. As I recall the day I went from thinking to knowing…Wow! What a day!

The adrenaline rush the day I began thinking of myself in a different, more positive, more successful light was absolutely phenomenal. I arrived at my first meeting as an official member!

My heart was beating so strong I thought for sure it would burst through my shirt like the S on Superman's chest. This meeting was going to be different. Instead of dreading running into my mentor because I hadn't officially started, I was looking for him. I had paid my fees, gotten my application into the home office and had enough knowledge to hit the pavement running. I was ready to take charge of my new life and I wanted my mentor to be the first to know.

Well, I found him, and quickly, I must say, told him the good news and received his congratulations.

"Carl," he said, "You stick with me over the next 90 days and you will never work another day in your life."

At that moment, I declared that in 90 days, I would be as successful as my mentor and I jumped in with both feet. I watched, I listened, I learned. I studied the materials, copied successful people and soon discovered what my Grandmother meant when she would say "The grasshopper that is always near its mother eats the best food." Staying near to my mentor taught me everything I needed to know and afforded me my first check within 30 days. I had gained a sense of purpose that still keeps me going to this day.

Finally I had arrived. Finally, I know what I want. Finally, I understand what success means to me and I am prepared to go out and get it, *finally*.

The business began to boom, and within 100 days of my start I was able to **fire** my boss of 12 years. Talk about a liberating experience!

I approached my mentor one Wednesday night after training and expressed my sincere gratitude. I could not have done it without him. He placed his hand on my shoulder, looked me straight in the eyes, and evoked the same power as he did at our first meeting.

> "Carl, my friend," he said "you don't have to thank me. I have to thank you. I travel the world sharing this very same information with thousands of people, but you took advantage of it and for that *I* am grateful.

Now go and multiply and impact humankind."

Wow! That was all I needed. I felt as though I had just received a brand new chance at life. At that moment I appreciated, embraced and took advantage of the opportunity to move forward with him for the next three years. I became a new person spiritually, mentally, physically professionally, and financially.

Between imitation and envy, imitation is better; between invention and duplication, duplication is always better – it already works!
~ *C. Anthony Harris*

Preparing for your journey...

Before you begin your journey to success, define what success means to you, decide to go after it and then put a few essential items in your bag.

- Pack a mindset for success. Remember, you are what you think!

- Take along a true mentor; a mentor you trust and respect; someone who will take the time to teach you what you don't know, what you need to know and possibly even bring to surface those things you already know but have buried in your subconscious.

- Don't forget to take along the accessories (Persistency, Consistency, Discipline Urgency and Excitement) necessary for the completion of your journey and by all means, take the faith in knowing that you can and you will reach your destination.

A True Mentor

I have to stress taking along a *true mentor* on your journey to success because any mentor won't do. A true mentor is someone who wants you to be successful; the mentor who would go to unimaginable lengths to help you become even more successful than him or herself. True mentors get a sincere gratification out of influencing and positively impacting others. After all, isn't that what God put us here to do-empower each other?

Take extreme care when choosing the mentor with whom you will travel. Think about it, you would not choose an unreliable car to drive across country, don't choose an unreliable mentor to travel through life.

In packing the accessories necessary to complete your journey take a sense of persistency, consistency, discipline, a high level of urgency and an overwhelming sense of excitement. Don't take that pair of shoes that doesn't match the outfit simply because they are comfortable. Success is not always comfortable but it's worth the pain in the end.

Lastly, pack that awesome outfit for the gala celebration once you have arrived and then enjoy the fruits of your labor. Congratulations on your success!

Now, some of you may still be saying, " I hear you, I understand your point and I believe in its validity, but, I cannot think of anyone who embodies the characteristics of a *true mentor*." Trust me, I understand. Sometimes you just can't seem to find that right pair of shoes for the occasion. To you, I say, take advantage of and receive the spirit in which this book was written.

As the author, I have accepted it as my duty, my responsibility and my purpose to empower others in creating the same type of success that I have been blessed to experience. If you don't have a true mentor, I will be your mentor.

The principles in this book have changed my life, my family's life and countless others who have come in contact with my training and began Living The Five Wealth Principles. Believe in the power of the Universe, yourself and then, hit the ground running. What do you have to lose? What do you have to gain – *SUCCESS*.

Believe in yourself, as I do. Affirm to yourself "Because I am a winner, I refuse to lose." Let go of the past clichés, myths, bad habits, negative thinking, failures, discouragement and disappointment, become coachable, teachable, and moldable. Make the decision and stay committed to changing your way of life. Learn, believe, internalize and begin Living The Five Wealth Principles and success is inevitable. You can and you will win!

PERSISTENCY

Cowards run when the storm hits, bravehearts weather it. ~ *C. Anthony Harris*

As a child, I am sure you had the experience of wanting something really badly. Whatever it was you wanted, you had to have it and would do almost anything to get it. You know how the story goes. You wanted to do something, go somewhere, have something that everyone else had. You asked your parents and they said no. You pleaded with them, you negotiated with them, cried, screamed, acted a fool and maybe even tried to challenge your dad because of this "thing" you had to have or had to do. You became angry and might have even threatened to runaway if you didn't get it and you definitely mumbled to yourself, "I can't wait to get out of here, and then I can do whatever I want." Whether you were successful in getting that "thing" or not, the point is that you were practicing persistency while trying to get it.

Your quest for success is now that "thing" you would give up anything and risk everything to get. Success, just like that "thing" will not come easy, it never has and it never will. Consequently, if you really want success, you have to become and remain persistent until you get it.

Let's review this principle closely.

Persistency

The verb persist means to refuse to give up, to continue insistently, to endure, to remain. In order for you to be successful at anything you do, you must fully understand the definition and immerse yourself into a state of being that will not allow you to give up; a state of being that will push you to continue insistently, to endure and to remain, until you get what it is you want. You must embody persistence and live by its principles and you must develop a level of persistency in your life that is outside of what has been the norm.

Outside of the norm...

Maintaining a level of persistency that is outside the realm of your norm requires work and determination. The more action you take toward becoming successful, the more persistent you must become. Refusing to give up must become as natural and as normal as the effort you make to tie your shoes. You have to develop a will power much like Ted Turner. One that is stronger than your tendency to give up when things don't go exactly as planned.

Ted Turner

In 1984, Turner envisioned the idea that broadcasting news 24 hours a day would be of interest to the public. He created a business plan for his idea and then went out in search of investors and the right people to back it. The first stop was ABC Networks.

When Turner presented his proposal, ABC turned him down. This was quite a disappointment for Ted. ABC, at the time, was the #1 television station in the nation and logic said that if they would buy into the idea, other networks would surely follow. Unfortunately, they did not see it that way.

He approached NBC Networks. They turned him down, telling him that he was crazy. People would not be interested in watching news 24 hours a day.

Because Ted was persistent, he went on to solicit support from the CBS Network. Mind you, by now, CBS had already heard that ABC and NBC had turned him down.

> If the road you take is a dead end, choose another!
> ~ Dad

What is it you think they did?
That's right, they too turned him down.
Ted, however, refused to give up, continued insistently, endured and remained focused until his thoughts became realities.

Stop for a minute and look at the dynamics of this scenario. If you were walking in Ted's shoes, what would have been your response?

Here you have three broadcast television giants turning down an opportunity to inform the world. Your idea is insensitively being crushed. They're telling you it will never work and dismissing you as if *you* were the idiot. What would you have done?

Would you have continued to be persistent or would you have simply accepted and believed their ideology? After all, they have many more years of experience and should have a pretty good idea of what works and what does not. Would you have doubted yourself? Began to think, that maybe you *were* crazy? Would you have thrown in the towel on your dreams, goals and desired outcomes or continued to pursue them? Not quite sure? Well, I'll tell you.

A great number of people would have given up. They would have settled into all of the negativity and not only would they not have continued to pursue that particular dream, many of them may not have ever gotten up the nerve to pursue anything else. Because it is so much easier to be negative than it is to be positive, many people would have quit the game before getting started.

It is definitely less of a headache to throw in the towel on any of your dreams and goals, than it is to tough it out and go for the gold one more time. Although it may be difficult to be like Ted Turner who did not take the easy road, it's definitely worth it in the end.

Ted, you see, went for the gold one more time, and came up with the idea of forming his own network for his 24-hour news broadcasts. We know it today as CNN and one of the most well respected news broadcasts of all time.

Today CNN provides news worldwide, and guess what, it even provides news coverage to those three networking giants ABC, NBC and CBS. Yes, those same networks that turned Ted Turner down, now purchase news from his network! Talk about your enemies becoming your footstools!

Not only that, some of the top anchor persons and news correspondents who got their beginnings at the other networks now work with Ted Turner and CNN.

> Strong souls have will power, weak ones desire power.
> ~ Granny

Persistency as with all of the five wealth principles must be internalized, lived and practiced every single day. You must become relentless in your quest for success and willing to stop at nothing until you achieve it.

Despite the pain of rejection, the agony of feeling defeated, the sweat of hard work, and the tears from the grief you get from those who do not believe you can do it, you must hold firmly to your dream, never let go or let up and absolutely never give in. No obstacle can stop a persistent person. Take it a step further and pursue your goals for success like Ted Turner, The Terminator, Michael Jordan or anyone who exemplifies the definition of persistence for you.

> You can create a new life by modeling it after one that has already lived.
> ~ C. Anthony Harris

    Developing an extraordinary level of persistency in your life may be easy for some and difficult for others but it can and it must be done. The good news, you don't have to try to do it alone. There are countless examples of people who exemplify persistence in our lives, in the news, and through the entertainment we enjoy. Choose one or two that help define persistency for you and copy their traits. Here's an example to help you get started.

    Remember the movie, The Terminator? Arnold Schwarzeneger was relentless in pursuing Miss Connor and he never stopped, regardless of all the obstacles he encountered. He walked through walls, fire, and even through explosions in order to succeed at his mission. He was focused on the prize and was willing to stop at nothing until he got it. The Terminator was persistent and you must become persistent as well. The most valuable lessons learned are those learned through the experiences of others.

> A blacksmith in one village becomes a blacksmith's apprentice in another.
> ~ *South African Proverb*

    I learned the art of persistency from a myriad of successful and powerful people, Michael Jordan, in particular.

    Jordan, if you recall, was persistent in winning the game of basketball and was unstoppable. Whenever he saw his opponent gaining on him, he would switch his game plan, shake them up, confuse them with his moves and still make it to the basket and score. He was persistent in his efforts to score. His entire focus was on scoring points and how he did it was not important; *that* he did it was. If he had to take a different route, so be it, but no matter what, he made the score, he practiced persistency.

Your success depends upon this type of persistency. How you get to your success is not as important as you actually getting there. You must embody the same type of determination as did Michael Jordan. Think about it. Oftentimes Jordan's determination in scoring caused him to have to "fly", as much as it is humanly possible, to the basket. The image of him soaring through the air to make the basket later became an icon synonymous not only with his name, but with success and is now recognized all over the world. You know the symbol.

Understand that the power of persistency taps into your creativity. Your desired outcome is success, but how you get there along with the sacrifices you are willing to make give birth to a strong attitude of persistency, a winning spirit, will power and an unstoppable determination.

Persistency Can Be Your Best Friend...

In my own experience, I vividly remember how persistency became my best friend and the very first time I had a breakthrough. It was in one of my business ventures with a fast growing company, I held the top position in the company, and was doing well.

I was consistently ranking as one of the top five producers of the company in all categories and performing in the top five percentile of the entire company was great. For me, however, my performance was still not good enough. Success for me was not defined by ranking at #4 or #5 and never achieving the position of #1 or #2.

Honestly, in the beginning I was very content with my rank. In my mind, I had settled for 4th and 5th position because even in those positions I had still achieved a great amount of success. After all, ranking four or five in a company of over 100,000 was pretty darn good, I thought. Then I began to observe the guy who was ranked #1. At that point my whole outlook changed.

I thought to myself, he's not any better than I am. What was he doing that I was not? As I have said before, it is always good to get the information you want straight from the horse's mouth and that's exactly what I did. I took advantage of the opportunity and I studied him closely. I took him out to lunch, spoke to him over the phone and spent as much time as possible picking his brain and gathering information that would help me to attain an even higher level of achievement. To my surprise he was just like my 25 year-old mentor. His secret, he like my mentor refused to take no for an answer. He refused to settle for the #2 spot and always kept his focus on the #1 position in the company.

The Observation

I quietly began to watch this guy on a regular basis. After observing him for a while and compiling my data, I decided to give him a challenge. I began to mimic his behavior and began my pursuit of the number one spot in the company. I made a commitment, first to myself, and then to my mentor. I made a vow to work harder and smarter and to ignore any fear of stumbling blocks, naysayers and even my own doubts.

I frequently reviewed the reward for hitting the #1 spot. I visualized what it would feel like, smell like, taste like, be like and what I would do once I achieved it. After enjoying my daydreams, I wrote down my goal and my desired outcome. I created a concise, fully detailed time-line with specific tasks to be completed. I prayed on it and put it to the Universe.

I declared my goal and my desired outcome, daily, in front of the bathroom mirror morning, noon, and night. Then, I went to work like a laser beam, with confidence, strength and power.

The Outcome

The second quarter ended and I was eager and excited to review my position report. To my disappointment and after all of the imagination, preparation, and declaration of my success, hard work and persistence, I still ended up #2.

Everyone praised me with sincerity for my efforts. They were so impressed with my fortitude. But, I was not. I was disappointed. Then I realized, even though I did not make it to #1, through my own persistence, I had moved closer to my goal and changed my former positions by as much as three levels. Although not good enough to satisfy my hunger for the #1 position, the accomplishment was a very tasty appetizer.

I may not have become what I wanted, but I was sure glad that I was not what I had been. Because I had taken the time to define success as the #1 position, I was able to see my progression towards it.

The Speech

When given the podium to make my acceptance speech as the #2 winner, I refused to let my feelings of defeat overpower me. With the desire to reach my goal of becoming #1 boiling inside of me, I announced that I would be back to take the #1 spot next quarter. I boldly told the crowd that this event would be the current holder of the #1 title's last time there and I challenged him to enjoy it while it lasted. I was taking his spot and keeping it!

Everyone thought I was nuts, and the heat was on. The tension grew thick and the battle for the next 90 days began that night. After leaving the podium, I remember thinking, "What the hell have I done?" I could not believe my actions. Now I would have to own up to my challenge or swallow my pride next quarter. My zealous attitude had created a war zone and not just with my competitors, but with myself.

> What suffices for a small project won't do for an enormous one.
> ~ *Author unknown*

    I went back to the drawing board, reviewed the things I had done well, made a list of the things that I did not do so well, the things I neglected to do and the areas where I could improve. I mapped out a game plan and began execution immediately. The first 30 days I failed miserably. Everything went wrong. Believe me, unexpected happenings seemed to camp out at my doorstep. However, with each negative hit, I grew more persistent.
    You see, I had a purpose. I had a goal. I had something that was very near and dear to me, something I was willing to do anything and everything to protect – my reputation. Not only was my reputation on-the-line but also my integrity, my word and most important, my promise to the most important person in the world, me! Consequently, I became even more persistent at achieving my goal.

I remained focused and never took my eyes off of the prize and the next sixty days were a breeze. As new obstacles presented themselves, I met them at the gate with resilience. As setbacks occurred, my sense of purpose and persistency grew even stronger. I was even more determined to endure until the end.

It seemed as though this challenge that I created for myself was the hardest battle I had ever encountered. Whenever the thought of defeat came into my mind, I would quickly replace it with thoughts of winning. Whenever I thought I was finished for the day, I would push myself to work a little longer. I worked on this project, day in and day out. My friends and family thought I was going nuts, that I was taking this challenge too far. But, I stayed focused. I woke up earlier, and went to bed later and I continued this routine up until the final hour of the competition.

The Final Hour

The final hour of the competition had come. I was sweating buckets. I was nervous, afraid of defeat and in doubt about whether or not I had put in enough work or even if I deserved to be [#]1. Then it was announced.

"C. Anthony Harris [#]1 Platinum Member for the quarter."

I had finally achieved the [#]1 position! All of the blood, sweat, tears, hard work, aggravation, sleepless nights, headaches, determination and persistence that put me there had finally paid off. Trust me words cannot explain the sense of accomplishment I felt. I had confirmed to myself that I could do anything to which I set my mind.

With persistency on my side I could not and I did not lose. I was feeling so high, I felt like a kid at Christmas. I felt so good about myself and my accomplishments; the rewards, the prizes, the trophy, and even the income that came with the position did not matter. What mattered most was that I had defined success for myself, believed that I could achieve it, declared that I would achieve it and had actually attained my desired outcome.

That day was a new beginning for me. My persistency helped me to grow into a better person, stay focused, endure until the end and set higher standards of performance for myself.

I remained at the #1 position for two additional quarters and in more than one category. The entire experience taught me that in order to have success in my life I had to become synonymous with it. I had to do what it took to get it. After all, to whom much is given, much is required.

Persistency And You

If you want success, you must adopt and develop a high regard for persistency. You must embody an attitude of persistency and govern yourself accordingly. You have to live and incorporate this wealth principle in every area of your life and strive toward your goal with vigor.

It's not forensic science people. There is no mystery behind becoming successful, achieving your goals and making things happen. The key is to become persistent, to hold steadfastly to your purpose as if your life depended upon it.

Be mindful, though, that it cannot be just any purpose. You have to find a purpose that means the world to you; a purpose driven by you inner spirit; a purpose that you are willing to die for; a purpose that will make your obstacles mere stepping stones to a brighter, more stable and prosperous future.

The Examples

Today both Michael Jordan and Ted Turner are retired from careers they relentlessly pursued. Their persistency has allowed them to reap lavish benefits and create wealth for generations to come. Their attitudes and life application of persistency has not only impacted their lives for the better, but thousands of others who live by their example as well.

Through their persistency, Ted Turner and Michael Jordan have produced everything from jobs to investors to millionaires who wanted to be just like them, copied their success and yes, became millionaires.

The Apple of Your Eye

Having understood that it takes persistency to achieve success, I urge you to keep your eyes on your prize, your goals, and your desired outcomes. Do not look at the hurdles, the setbacks, the cuts, or the pain you may go through on your journey to success. Adversity is designed to strengthen you. What does not kill you will only make you stronger. You have to keep pressing toward your mark.

> In due season, the seeds you plant will reveal their growth.
> ~ Granny

While you may never have realized it before now, you have at some point in your life employed persistency and practiced it until you got your desired outcome. Think about it.

Remember the time when you were pursuing the apple of your eye. You know the one, that young man or young lady you met at a party, at school, at work, or even at church. Remember the spirit of attraction that came over you; that little voice thumping on your heart-strings saying "I've got to have him or her." From the time the desire was initiated, you began to think of ways you could win that person over, the "seeds" you could plant about yourself that would make this person grow to… let's start at like you.

All sorts of things ran through your mind.

How did you feel? Were you challenged? Excited? Afraid of the risk? Nervous?

I'm certain to some degree, you were all of those things and more, but what did you do? If you are anything like me, you relentlessly pursued that person. You picked the best "seeds" about yourself, watered them with a little flattery and went home praying like crazy they would take root and grow into a…let's start at friendship.

You did not care what your mother, your dad, your friends, or siblings had to say. You did not care how much it would cost to impress this person or how much time it would take, as long as you got the prize. You wanted this person, you were willing to do whatever it took to have them and you were persistent. You did not take no as the answer and you were successful in your quest.

It is this type of determined, elevated, out-of-the-norm level of persistence required for achieving success. Make success the apple of your eye and go after it with everything you've go. Become the Tom that has been chasing Jerry for the last thirty or forty years in the popular cartoon Tom & Jerry. You remember the cat and mouse.

For over three decades Tom has been trying to catch Jerry. In his pursuit he has had things dropped on him, suffered broken bones, spent time devising plan after plan, and in one episode he was even electrocuted. The point is Tom never stopped trying. It's been thirty years and Tom still has not captured Jerry but he's still trying.

Again, it's not rocket science. Success is attainable. Anyone who accepts the challenge to begin live Living the Five Wealth Principles can and will be successful.

Are you persistent? Do you have what it takes to become persistent? Not sure?

The following five questions and exercises can help you determine your level of persistence.

1. Name one goal you have achieved because of your persistence.
2. Name five areas in your occupation in which you are persistent.
3. List five areas in your personal development where you are persistent.
4. When confronting adversity/obstacles, how do you respond?
5. Where do you see persistence fitting into your life, as a partner or as a mundane chore? Explain.

If you are not satisfied with your current level of persistency in life, use the strategies that follow to help you increase.

If you are satisfied with your current level of persistence, always remember that successful people always work to improve themselves. Use the strategies that follow to enhance your persistency.

Go through each strategy, carefully, truthfully and with a sense of purpose. Success is there for you to take, it will not be given to you.

The strategies will assist you in moving to the next dimension of persistency in your life, put into practice and experience the benefits of Living The Five Wealth Principles. Enjoy!

Living The Five Wealth Principles LifePlan Persistency Strategies for Success ™

1. Think through and write down your goals and the desired outcome for each. What is it that you truly desire? How do you define success? What do you expect to gain from pursuing a certain goal? Be very specific in your answers. Date your thoughts and then form a contract with yourself bonding your commitment to achieving your goals. Don't just think it, believe it!

2. Revisit your list of goals and prioritize them in order of importance to you. Before you move on any of the things you've listed, bless them! Offer your goals and desired outcomes to The Universe, the power higher than humankind and exercise faith in knowing that they will, in time, come to pass.

3. Visualize your success everyday. Every minute you can get, take time

to meditate on it. See it in your mind's eye.

4. Find a trusted counselor (a true mentor) who will keep you on track and make you accountable, keep you to your word. Make sure that you are truthful and honest and communicate with him or her daily.

5. Do not share your goals/results with anyone who cannot help or encourage you to achieve your success. Others may not have the same vision as you. Those who do not share your vision will remind you of your failures, throw pity parties for you, and ultimately destroy your dream before it becomes a reality.

6. Declare your goal and desired outcomes out loud in front of a mirror. Look the most important person in the world-you, in the eye and declare your success! By verbally claiming ownership of your success you are, inadvertently, releasing and affirming it with the universe. Place your hand over your

heart, focus your mind, make eye contact and stare deep into your own eyes and recite your declaration. Be truthful with yourself and understand that this exercise will make you nervous and uncomfortable. Only when we begin to look, communicate and be truthful with our inner-selves will confidence strengthen and power move us from the belief that we can be successful to the comfort of knowing we are successful.

7. Be, Do, Have ~ Most people want to have success but are not willing to become or do whatever it takes to get it. Do not make this mistake. In order to become successful you, first, have to embody success. Make a list of the characteristics of successful people. Study the behaviors, the habits, the conversations, and the extra-curricular activities of successful people. Did you know that a great majority of business deals are made on the golf course? Start doing, participating, and practicing some of the things successful people do. You know the saying, "When in Rome do

as the Romans do." Experience success before you actually achieve it and you will know how to handle it. You will afford yourself the opportunity of not only mastering the game, but also appreciating it. Your experiences prior to success will teach you humility and keep you grounded. Once success begins to happen for you, you can be relaxed and positive, not cocky, arrogant or ignorant.

8. Celebrate small successes. Don't wait for the grand finale. Keep your eyes on the prize but do not fail to acknowledge those things that contribute to the big picture. Whenever you accomplish a small success, treat yourself. Reward yourself for your accomplishment. When you work hard, you must play and reward hard. Small celebrations make your journey to success fun and invigorating. Have fun with it.

9. Feed your mind. Read about high achievers, winners, and/or successful people at least once per week. Reading wide varieties of success

stories is a great way to model your own success. Learning from other high achievers can be one the most powerful lessons you can gain for pennies on the dollar. Successful people love sharing how they got there. When you read about the journeys of others you unlock clues that will help you build your success and help you to avoid pitfalls of failure. Reading this material will also ease your anxiety. You will see that success is not an overnight accomplishment. You don't go to bed one night, decide you want to become successful and wake up the next morning successful. You have to put in your time, blood, sweat, and tears the same way others before you have done. Feeding your mind with this material will keep you encouraged.

10. Write out a Daily-to-Do List. This area is simple but not easy. Writing down your daily list of activities and using it as a guide, keeps you on point, organized, accountable and focused on what is important. The best part is actually scratching out a

task on your to-do-list once completed. No matter how small the task, you will feel some sense of accomplishment once it's completed. This habit is extremely important. As you become more successful you will have more to do. Your mind will be working overtime and you will need to write down that thought, task, or deadline. Forgetting to meet a deadline, submit a proposal or attend a function can sometimes mean the loss of millions of dollars or the opportunity to impact someone else's life or even your own.

12. Get a calendar, monitor and track your progress daily. As you force yourself to produce, chart your goals and desired outcomes in the following order.

30	Days
60	Days
90	Days
6	Months
1	Year

Words of Caution

- Do not fall prey to the ignorance of naysayers.
- Naysayers view persistence as obsession, insanity and will tell you, in the face of adversity, not to continue your pursuit. They will tell you to cut your losses and move on; to give up.
- Naysayers will label you as a fairytale, a dreamer, a fanatic, and maybe even a fool.
- Stay away from people who do not understand your vision.
- Avoid jealous people who will try to hinder you because they have not had the drive to pursue their own dreams.
- Stay away from skeptics. They will try to convince you that your program does not work or that they have a better deal. They will not take the time to find out what your vision is. Don't waste time trying to explain.
- Be prepared to be seen as insensitive, stubborn, unsociable, and even selfish by those closest to you.

- Your confidence will often be mistaken as arrogance. Do not diminish it for the sake of others.
- Begin to practice and live the wealth principle of persistency, add on the principle of consistency and you are well on your way to success.

At the end of this chapter, I have identified my mentors and a few high achievers who exemplify persistency for me. All of them to some degree have helped me to understand, respect and live the wealth principle of persistency. They all embody admirable characteristics driven by their persistence and by studying, learning and mimicking their behaviors, you can dramatically change your life. You might have something in common.

While we may have some in common, take the time to personalize your own list and identify the persistency they practice. Through your success become an inspiration to someone else.

C. Anthony Harris
Donald Trump
Quincy Jones
Wendy Mandela
Ted Turner
Bruce Lee
Mary J. Blige
Toni Braxton
Lee Iococa
Tom of Tom & Jerry
Samuel L. Jackson
P. Diddy
Lance Armstrong
Jamie Foxx
Denzel Washington

Oprah Winfrey
Maya Angelou
Michael Beckwith
Coretta Scott King
Barack Obama
Lisa Nichols
Michael Jordan
Popeye the Sailor
Will Smith
Henry Ford
Russell Simmons
Tina Turner
Muhammad Ali
Hillary Clinton

Who are the icons of persistency in your life?

_____
_____
_____
_____
_____
_____
_____
_____

CONSISTENCY

The light that is plugged into its energy source shines the brightest.
~ *Reality*

The first step toward success, we know is persistency. Persistency, however, is nothing without its power source – CONSISTENCY. There are no if's, and's or but's about it. If you really want success, it is mandatory that you embrace persistency while maintaining a level of consistency in everything that you do.

The Energy Source

When you plug anything into an electrical outlet or "power source" there is a certain level of energy that must consistently move through the current in order for the light, TV, appliance, or whatever it is to work properly. If ever the current is interrupted the performance diminishes or stops completely. It's the same with your quest for success. If you are not *consistently persistent* you will diminish or totally stop your progression.

Once you have decided that success is the only option for you, you have to be consistent and persistent in your efforts to achieve it. Otherwise, all of the outside elements that have enough energy to exert negative power surges into your life, your dreams and your goals will cause your system for success to fail.

You must produce and maintain an electrifying current of consistency in your efforts to achieve success and allow it to flow through your life, daily.

By Definition

Webster's dictionary defines consistency as the: cohesiveness, firmness, agreement or harmony in parts of different things, and uniformity (~ of behavior). Though all of the definitions are meaningful, in relationship to success, "uniformity in behavior", for the purposes of this book, is most suitable.

Understanding the true meaning of consistency, is the development and practice of uniform behavior and believe me, it's not as hard as you think. In fact, you do it everyday without much effort. Take a look at all of the many things we do as human with, consistency.

Consistency, It's Only Natural

Life. Every minute of the day, you and I practice consistency without any effort. How?...by breathing. That's right, the practice of this principle is as simple and as natural as the breath we take to survive. To live and to continue living we must and we do it ever so unconsciously and we do it with consistency.

Work. We go to work with consistency. Successful people do not go to work and do eight hours only when we feel like it. Because work provides finances, we do eight hours with a consistency that yields a full paycheck. At the end of the day, we go home, come back the next day, and go back again. We practice the same routine with consistency.

Eating. Eating is something we do with consistency. The consistency with which we eat for some of us may be over the top, but we do it nevertheless. When we decide to lose the excess, we practice consistency in exercise and diet. We watch more closely what we eat. Those who don't, experience negative health problems as a direct result of their consistency in practicing bad eating habits.

The Heart. Our hearts pump blood with a certain level of consistency 24 hours a day, 365 days a year at a rate that is steady and tuned just right to the idiosyncrasies of our individual bodies. Until that consistency is interrupted and we die, the heart never stops beating. Get my point?

Consistency and You

When looking at the wealth principle consistency, understand that uniformity in behavior as well as the law of repetition is vital to your success. You must begin to practice routine behaviors that contribute to achieving the goals you have set for yourself and the persistency you have developed. The synergy between consistency and persistency is important because you will not achieve the success you desire if you are persistent today, slacking tomorrow, doing what worked yesterday and trying something new today. You must develop a uniform behavior and the attitude that you will become successful and nothing and no one will stop you from reaching your goal.

Where Did My Attention Go?

Consistency was always a problem for me. Even now, I sometimes struggle with it. After being blessed with so many wonderful experiences, my attention span can go very quickly. I get excited about so many things and want to do them all. Before discovering how to change my circumstances through Living The Five Wealth Principles, it was this principle that often had me disheartened.

Project, After Project After...

Through the second wealth principle, consistency, I learned that my feelings of hopelessness were coming from my failure to finish what I had started. I would start project after project after project and never completed a one.

In a nutshell, whenever I began a new project, I began with excitement. I was persistent at getting it started but, whenever any part of what I started did not go as I had planned, I stopped. I quit. I was not consistent enough to weather the storm. I gave up. I would then wallow in my disappointment that the project failed as opposed to figuring out what I needed to do in order to make it work. Simply put, I lacked consistency.

I became bored with trying to make something work by doing it over and over and over. I did not understand that each time I did whatever it was over, I did it better than the last. I did not understand that my consistency would only improve my projects and if I just stayed with them, *something* would come out of my efforts. I continued this destructive cycle until I met my mentor.

My mentor taught me that consistency was an integral part of the foundation for success. I soon discovered that I was not a failure I was just not aware of the power behind consistency.

I had not developed the uniform habit of continuing with the projects I started and enduring until the end to ensure their success. I often waited for success to drop from the sky and found myself surprised when it didn't.

I, like many of you have and are thinking right now, thought all I had to do was come up with a great idea and the rest would take care of itself. After all, how could a great idea fail? Isn't a great idea supposed to hold its own?

After The Focus

After focusing my attention on the power of consistency, I finally had this thing figured out, or so I thought.
With the help of my mentor I began to focus and actually made progress in the area of consistency. I began to make lists. Develop daily routines that contributed to my success and plan my day down to the very second. The first three or four hours were enjoyable. My morning schedule consisted of all of the things I liked to do. After all, that's where we tend to put most of our attention- to the things we enjoy. The latter part of my day, however, was a monster.
In my efforts to become a better, more successful person, I would plan to use the second half of my day to complete the tasks that required my undivided attention. My thought was that if I got all of the other stuff out of the way, the rest of the day could be devoted solely to my success. WRONG!

The second half of my day was planned out to do things I really had to force myself to do. Because they were less interesting to me, consistency became a problem, again. I began to associate this ever so powerful principle with B-O-R-E-D-O-M.

How can anyone have fun doing the same thing over and over and over again? Where's the variety? Where's the excitement, the spice? It was this type of thinking that led to the demise of all of my "would be" successful projects. It was this type of thinking that caused me to become discouraged, disheartened, and down in the dumps. It was this type of thinking and the feelings it evoked that made me not only have to change but want to change and that's when I really began to heighten my sense of awareness for what other successful people were doing and oh, what a transformation.

When I really honed in on copying successful people I began to understand my boredom and find creative ways to channel it into productivity.

> Properly identify the problem, and you discover the right solution.
>
> ~ C. Anthony Harris

In my desire to really understand my problem with consistency, I had to do some real soul searching, and so will you. I discovered that my problems not only stemmed from the boredom often associated with repetition, but also with behaviors developed throughout childhood that I, until now paid no attention to and when I did- I thought they were normal.

It's All A Mindset

As children, our parents, care providers, teachers, friends, siblings, and/or neighbors took great strides in developing the proper mindsets by which we should live. With the intention of making us model citizens, more often than not, the first mindsets we learned dealt with teaching right from wrong, when to say no and when to stop doing unpleasant things.

These well thought out, predetermined "normal" ways of thinking were almost always based on what our parents thought were acceptable behaviors and became the foundation of what I like to call The Dad's National Anthem…you know the one that begins "The way we do things in this house…and ends with "As long as you live under, my roof, you'll do what I say."

In most cases, these mindsets were helpful. They helped us to determine how we should properly respond to and interpret every situation we encountered. Even today these mindsets, for most of us, continue to control our behaviors.

As children these mindsets determined our moral development; the "moral box" in which we lived. As adults, they sometimes determine our progression toward or regression from success. Let's examine this idea closely.

> You're probably thinking I am off of my rocker. Bare with me. Don't ask for a refund just yet. I haven't gone from success coach to insanity in one chapter. There is a point to all of this. You just keep reading and preparing for your ultimate success. I'm still on the journey, so stay with me.

No…Stop…Don't

Remember how we were taught right from wrong as children? In many instances "no", "stop" and "don't" were the first three words we learned. When we did not obey the command of these words, our backsides were met with a belt or the wood of a chair in the timeout corner. Over time we got the message and associated the words no, stop and don't with "pain", things we did not enjoy and we, eventually, ceased to continue the undesired behavior.

These same three words were used as we got older to develop our morals and values, thought processes and actions- the ways of the world, if you will, or more realistically, the ways of specific neighborhoods and individual families.

We were taught to live "right" according to a standard set of values or within a boxed set of rules and anything outside of that "moral box" was wrong. Consequently, whenever a venture outside of "the box" occurred, many of us heard "no…stop…don't do that" and the behavior, desire, dream, or goal had to cease. Why? Because our upbringing said so.

Oh, we may have tried to start our own business, begin a new career, or marry that man or woman the family didn't approve of, but at the first inclination of a problem, an obstacle or boredom associated with remaining consistent until our venture saw the light of day, we quit. We stopped the behavior, pursuit of the dream or goal, said no to the possibilities that lied outside of our comfort zone and/or simply did not do it. Remember that project you dropped?

If your memory's still a little foggy, the questions below may help you to at least entertain the idea that the "moral boxes" in which we were raised, to a degree, control our behaviors and affect our consistency.

- You want to write a book. Throughout your school days you got F's in English and writing composition. How in the world does a failing English student write a book?

- You grow up in a family of educators. Your parents are college professors and have been saving for your college tuition since before you were born. Education is all you know. Do you really have a choice about going to college or not?

- Your family believes in good, honest, hard work and job security. Everyone in your family has held the same job for the last 30 years and they are continuing in hopes of securing their social security. Will they ever understand or support entrepreneurship or the risks you take?

I discussed this ideology with my editor. I wanted to know if the topic was too over the top, too much in the "grey" area, if my readers would think I had lost my mind, if I should remove it from the book. She advised me to keep it. This is what she said,

> "It's good information but you have to find a way to explain it so people can relate. If they can relate, they can understand your point. Once they understand, they can begin the process of evaluating their own "moral boxes" and analyzing the effects they've had on their pursuit of success or lack of".

As an entrepreneur, I live in a "box" that dictates for me to seize worthy opportunities. My first thought was take the advice, go back to the drawing board and rewrite. My second thought was use your resources-ask her to give an example. What's the harm, the invoice is pretty thick already. As a success coach, however, I was truly mesmerized by her eloquent response. I had to know what her response would be if she analyzed her own "moral box."

I went back to the drawing board. Rewrote the piece and then popped the question. No, not that "question". I didn't ask her to marry me. I asked her and I ask you,

> "If you were to look back at the decisions you have made in your life, how has the "moral box" in which you were raised influenced your choices?" Have you ever stepped outside of your "moral box"? If so, how did you feel? Were you more successful within or outside of your "moral box"?

Her Response

My editor explained, the words no, stop and don't, had a great influence on the choices and decisions she made in her life. These words kept her out of trouble and on a straight and narrow path. But, was that path too narrow for the success she desired for her life? Let's see.

My "moral box" had a tremendous effect on the choices and decisions I made in my life. In retrospect, I think that the rules I was brought up to live by kept me out of trouble but in some ways kept me from being me; from exploring my creativity, leadership and my personal goals for success.

My future was planned for me. The formula was this:
High school +College (A good job) = A financially secure and happy life!

It didn't happen!

Although she had a burning desire to become a successful entrepreneur, she always felt bound to her "moral box" and never even entertained the idea until much later in life. Her box, you see, had very defined sets of rules about what was acceptable and what was not. Starting a business and not going to college was never an option.

> As a pretty intelligent student in high school, I was in the CLASS -Collegiate Level Advancement something or another program designed for college bound students. The "other" students as they were often referred were sent to the career center where they learned a variety of trades.
>
> It seemed as if they had so much fun. They were learning to do things with their hands, to become entrepreneurs, and to explore their creativity while my head was buried in a Calculus book.
>
> In my home, it was never *if* you go to college, only which one would you like to attend and even those options were limited.
>
> My dream of becoming a successful entrepreneur at the time was kept at that-a dream.
>
> In my "moral box" the rules were up in lights and I was reminded of what I should be working towards daily. They stated "Corporate America" or "Law School," that's it!

I asked if she ever tried to negotiate, find compromises to or even suggest alternatives to the rules that governed her moral box and that's when it all began to unfold. Anything that met the approval of or was acceptable within her "moral box" she tried; anything that challenged or required her to step outside of her box, she avoided.

> I have always had this burning desire to open my own interior design business. That's not what I have my degrees in but it has always been my passion.
>
> I mentioned this once to a family member, whose home I decorated by the way and the response went something like this.
>
> You don't know anything about that. You'd better keep your day job. You need stability. You're too old to be trying to get into owning your own business. Don't you know you have to work towards your retirement, your pension? Why are you willing to give up a definite for a possibility? Stop dreaming and get real!"

Discouraged and afraid of the rejection she would feel if she "rocked the box"; my editor never ventured outside of it and never challenged the rules that had begun to suppress her enthusiasm, her creativity and the desires she had for her life. She began to settle for what life was giving in an effort to please those around her and she was miserable.

> As I look back on that time in my life, I see now that I was miserable. I was always seeking the approval of those I loved but never satisfying myself. I was very unhappy. I was bored out of my mind.
>
> I worked job, after, job after, after, job; all of which I worked to meet the approval of my "moral box"...you know the ones with the big fancy titles. In all of my due diligence, however, I still did not meet the mark.

She began to seek jobs that would meet the approval of her parents, even though they made her miserable. Because she was so miserable, once she got bored, she would find another, get bored, find another and another and the cycle continued. Her efforts in landing great jobs were never recognized-only her failure to keep them made the family reunion newsletter. Her parents were never satisfied.

Moving from job to job would never build the seniority necessary for a pension. After all, she was expected to work with consistency to prove her eligibility for "social security." Her parents thought she just couldn't cut the mustard.

Every time I quit a job. I heard it!

> How could you do such a thing? Don't you know there are a million people who would love to have the job you just quit? I am disappointed in you. Grow up!

Well, I was more disappointed in myself. My parents stayed on their jobs twenty, thirty years and I could not manage to maintain enough consistency to make it more than a year. I would sit and wonder-Why me?

And then I met you! Hooray! All hail to C. Anthony Harris and Living The Five Wealth Principles!

Through Living The Five Wealth Principles, my editor discovered that what she lacked was not potential nor was it staying power. It was consistency. She also discovered that her lack of consistency stemmed from the boredom she experienced with being confined in her "moral box." She learned that in order to really be successful in life, she had to begin defining what success meant for her and stop living her life "According to Jim". Living inside the dreams and aspirations of others always made her fear disappointing them and ultimately caused her to disappoint herself. Now that she knows better, she is doing better.

She has now begun to explore her interior design business and is well on her way to the life she's always wanted.

> You know, when you asked me the question about my moral box, I must admit, I was afraid to answer. I thought I would, again, discover some deep dark secret about my inadequacies. But, now that I have a clearer understanding about what success means to me, I know I have what it takes.
>
> You'll be happy to hear, I have begun to research interior design schools and I am preparing to open my own business; only this time I am going to stick with it. I will make it happen. I won't stop until I do.

I strongly urge you not to make the same mistake. Don't live your life according to Jim. Remember, success is relative and the only way to attain it is to first define what it means to you. Then, pursue that goal, that woman or man, that business, that burning desire inside of you with everything you've got. Go after it with a persistency and a consistency that moves like a freight train with no brakes. *Keep m-o-v-i-n-g!*

Are You still with me? I told you I'd get there. Let's continue.

> Everyone has his or her own way of dressing a chicken, in the end, only the taste matters.
> ~
> *Granny*

If boredom is not your problem with maintaining consistency in your life, what about worry, doubt or fear? When I get to yours, just highlight!

No One Person Plays The Game The Same

Not everyone is inconsistent because they are bored. Some of us may lack consistency because our attention is focused on worry, doubt and fear and not on the uniform behaviors that lead to success. Think about it. What are the behaviors associated with worry, doubt, and fear? That's right…depression, complacency and ultimate self-destruction.

Lack of consistency related to worry, doubt or fear, can be related to the negative circumstances and influences in our lives. In the example with my editor, her parent's had positive intentions in their installation of right and wrong in her life.

Let's get out of the "politically correct box" and take a look at the other side of the spectrum. What are the effects of no, stop and don't in an environment where positive reinforcement is lacking?

The Other Side Of The Spectrum

In homes where positive reinforcement is an un-welcomed stranger, the words no, stop and don't block consistency and in some instances limit the growth of success.

People who become engulfed in negative surroundings often lack consistency because they feel that they cannot rise above their circumstance. They worry about things they cannot control. They doubt their own abilities and fear the very thought of success because it is not the norm in their lives.

Some who are affected by negative environments get caught up in a web of fear because they are afraid of what their peers will think. They don't want to be accused of "forgetting where they come from" or being a "goody two-shoes', you know, "turning their back on the hood".

I spoke with a high school teacher who makes it even clearer.

I have many students who lack consistency because of the negative circumstances in their lives.

Some of the experiences these students go through are unimaginable and downright cruel.

They come to school one week, maybe two, and sometimes just to get away. But, the minute they get into a fight, are required to do something more than nothing, or experience something they don't like-they stop coming.

The consistency or inconsistency in attendance and effort seems to be determined by whatever they are experiencing in their personal lives at the time which most of the time is not good.

Even my better students would rather skip class if the gang is banging that day. The way they see it; they can't turn their back on the hood…that's where their loyalty lies and they do have to go home *after* school.

Others have been controlled by their parents' fear of failure. They may start a project but fail to complete it because, ironically, their success actually disappoints their parents or even makes them angry. They are never encouraged to do anymore than what their parents have done in life but very often discouraged. Take a look.

> I spend a lot of time encouraging my students to get an education and work towards getting into a good college.
>
> I thought I was doing a good thing. You know, what I was supposed to do as a teacher.
>
> One day, I met a parent who was adamantly against her son going to college. I could not understand why so I asked. She told me he could not go to college because she never went. She got pregnant as a teen and spent her time raising him. There was no way she would allow him to do what she had not. He became her excuse for not going to college and the excuses snowballed from there.

    Sometimes, those who have struggled so long with adversity in their everyday lives develop a sense of loyalty to the "hood", to their failures and to their hopelessness. They thrive on and sustain their being through negative impulse and have no clue about how to turn things around. They fear change; the unknown. They worry about not being able to compete in positive environments and they doubt their abilities. Some never free themselves of this bondage. Others do, but it takes an extremely rude awakening before they actually see the big picture. The movie "Animal" illustrates this point.

Animal

In the film the main character, Animal, made a name for himself on the street. He made money illegally and was famous as a notorious gangster inside prison walls as well as on the outside.

While in prison, Animal meets a *true mentor*, someone he trusts, confides in and communicates with on a regular basis. He turns his life around and embraces the opportunity to live a wholesome life upon his release.

Animal's son, who has been raised by his grandmother, grew up in the shadows of his father's notorious behavior. Negative circumstances became his parents and the only way of life for him. Selling drugs and gang-banging was actually normal. His "moral box" was built on criminal activity, immoral behavior and finding ways to challenge and beat "the system". If he sold drugs and got away with it, or even survived to see the next day, he was "successful" (only in his mind…) - he had beaten the system.

Upon Animal's release, he tries to prevent his son from making the same mistakes he did in his youth. His son, however, has chosen a life in the streets and is attracted to maintaining his father's notorious legacy. Although his father tries to teach him a more positive way of living, the new way challenges his norm and naturally, he refuses it.

He refuses to take the advice of his father because he worries about what will happen to his "reputation" as a true gangster. What will the "hood" think of his loyalty? Will he be seen as a coward? How can he actually participate in a moral society, when he's been in the habit of breaking laws instead of obeying them? How will he survive without an education? When other students were in school, he was on the corner hanging out.

In his "moral box" all he has ever been taught has been negative. Consequently, he is afraid to step out into the positive because he does not think he can do it and even more so he does not know how.

Animal's son doubts his ability to do anything outside of what he knows-the street: gang-banging and drug dealing. He fears failure, and subsequently, stays bound to the negative behavior that is his comfort zone. Not until a serious tragedy occurs does he begin to think differently.

At his apparent point of no return, Animal's son realizes the importance of his father's teachings and with consistency begins to reroute the direction of his life.

The LFWP Connection

The lack of consistency varies among the life experiences and the moral boxes in which we have been raised. It's easy for us all to practice consistency with the things we enjoy. However, whenever there is a challenge to what we believe, what we like, what has been normal for us or what we really desire, we lose the consistency in working towards our success. We lose it either out of boredom, or out of the fear, worry or doubt that we can actually achieve what we set out to accomplish.

The important point to remember is that life happens whether we like it or not.

As Bob Marley, put it "We have to face the day…come what may." With that said, we must make the most of it. We have to move through life with a persistency and consistency that benefits us in the end. It's going to take some work. But, as my grandfather would say "without effort, no harvest will be abundant".

The key is to prepare yourself for the day either you or fate decides that you have to change your life, your circumstance, and your future whether you want to or not. Prepare for that day by getting into a mindset that will allow consistency to take a front row seat. Develop a uniform set of behaviors that contribute to your success and keep moving toward you mark. Break away from the inhibitions created by no stop and don't. Write that book; open that business marry that woman or man and do what it takes to make it work-with consistency, of course.

If you have problems, regroup. Increase your level of consistency by copying successful people. Find hope in their stories and know, if we did it, so can you.

> Hope drives progress, fear prevents it.
>
> ~ C. Anthony Harris

Success to Copy

Copying successful people is the easiest way to learn. Through copying their behaviors you begin practicing what already works. They've done it. All you have to do is repeat it. Get ready, get set, and let's see who we can copy!

Tiger Woods

You don't have to be a golf fan to know that Tiger Woods is the King of Consistency! Just look at his record!
Since his first hole-in-one at the age of six, this golf legend has been not just winning but setting phenomenal records and he's been doing this with consistency for the past two and a half decades!

For twenty-five years Tiger Woods has practiced consistency in his game and has won numerous titles. If you look at his records you will see many of the titles he has won are consecutive.

At the age of 31 Tiger has won 75 tournaments including three (3) Masters. In 2001, he became the first player ever to hold all four professional major championships at one time and he was the first to win on the PGA tour *twice* in one year since 1990. He has been titled as the leading money winner on the PGA Tour. Even more impressive is his #1 world ranking in his 42nd week as a professional golfer. And that's not all.

Tiger Woods is the youngest *EVER* No. 1 golfer. He made the fastest rise to the top 100 in just six weeks, to the top 50 in just eight weeks and to the top 10 in just 33 weeks. That's less than a year!

How do you think he did it? Consistency! Somewhere, I speculate, Tiger mastered consistency. You can't make those kinds of records with that type of consistency without practicing…that's right, you're catching on…*CONSISTENCY.*

Whether it was in his practice, in his stroke, in his put, assessment of the course, in his concentration…wherever, somewhere,

Tiger Woods practiced consistency and continues to enjoy the success it brings.

He has a drive and a passion for the game that keeps him going. Where he's headed next I don't know. He's broken almost every record known to man. I can tell you this, wherever or whatever it is he will put his mind to doing next I would imagine it's probably a goal for success he has clearly defined.

Now, you might be saying "I have a desire, I am driven and I am determined. How is Tiger's drive for success any different than mine?"

I am glad you asked. It's not! Don't get caught up in the accomplishments of others and discourage yourself. Too many times I have coached people out of a slump after they've given up because they weren't number 1.

The key to copying successful people is to find out how they applied these wealth principles to get where they are and tailor their techniques to your specific goals.

You cannot increase your consistency through learning to play golf. You may not even like the game. What you can do is find out how many hours Tiger devoted to practice, how he prepared mentally and physically for the tournament, how he stayed focused, what techniques did he use to motivate himself to continue when or if he ever felt like giving up. Find out how consistent he was in doing these things. Copy that consistency and apply it to your quest for success.

    To increase your consistency, find something you like, something you are good at or want to become better at, something that drives your passion, something that at the end of the day will allow you to be proud of you and your accomplishments. Then practice the same type of consistency as did Tiger in getting it done.

    Your quest for success is no different than Tiger's, Donald Trump's, Oprah's or mine. The difference lies in *your* purpose. It's not the oven that makes the best cake, it's the batter. Your success has to be made with your ingredients. Let's look and learn from a few others whose consistency has brought them insurmountable success.

The Rolling Stones

Consistency must be practiced everyday. You have to develop positive habits in order to become successful and you have to do what works over and over and over and over again. When you don't feel like doing it, do it anyway. The Rolling Stones, for example, did not become a billion dollar band over the last three or four decades because they performed only when they felt like it.

Over the last 40 years the Rolling Stones have been consistently singing the same songs, and adding value to their performances. And, with consistency they are, 40 years later, still selling out concerts wherever they go.

They have developed a very strong sense of consistency through their commitment to wow their audience rain, sleet, snow or shine. Each time they perform they give just a little bit more and a little bit more and just a little bit more. They have created fans across the world that would literally travel across the world to see them because, while they never know what to expect, they can always count on a good show. Through their consistency in pleasing their fans, The Rolling Stones have evolved from a small town band into a billion dollar music industry phenomenon.

It is important to understand that they didn't begin their journey at their destination-ultimate success. They actually began with very humble beginnings and no real direction. However, they worked hard, tour after tour and developed uniformity in behavior and simply continued to do and perfect what worked over and over and over and over again. Today The Stones are no longer a small town band in England, but an international icon with private planes, trucks, massive equipment, sound systems, etc. What is their secret?

There is no secret. Mick Jagger and his crew looked for and put into practice ways they could improve their performance as well as their administrative operation. Traveling the world with about 200 employees required them to develop consistency in the way things were done. In order for the performances to be as close to perfection as possible, everyone had to understand their role and perform it with consistency.

It is this type of uniformity in behavior that landed The Rolling Stones a cover story with Forbes Magazine. The message conveyed- success begins with establishing a purpose and sticking to it.

It's simple. In order to put the principle of consistency into action in your life, all you have to do is stay with it. Whatever the project, goal, or ambition, work on it daily with consistency and you will get it done. Practice this principle everyday and soon it will become a part of your regular routine.

> **It's not the metal that makes the blacksmith great, it's the practice he gets in forging it.**
>
> ~ C. Anthony Harris

Because there is always room for improvement, I won't tell you that practice makes perfect, but it will definitely make positive progression towards your success. The more practice you get on a consistent basis, the more progress you make. Stay with me, there's more.

Consistency coupled with persistency develops the uniform behavior of professionals. In time, you no longer view your goals as unattainable dreams, but as money-making businesses or lifestyles that positively impact society.

Denzel Washington

To copy Denzel Washington is to copy not only success but consistency. Denzel worked as an actor for twenty years before he won an Oscar. Throughout the hard work, determination, and, at times, disappointment and discouragement, he never gave up.

Lance Armstrong

Lance Armstrong battled cancer and through consistency in eating right, exercising, and mentally preparing himself for the challenges he faced, won for the seventh consecutive time, the Tour de France.

C. Anthony Harris

Congratulations! You are now reading the story of yet another successful person you can copy. Me! I want you to know that everyone can win at the game of life it's all in how you execute your gameplan. This is how I won.

Remember my mentor, the 25 year-old millionaire? Well, whenever we would meet, he would always make the profound statement that if I would work with him for 90 days without interruption, I would never work another day in my life. Because he was so confident and consistent with this affirmation, I decided to take him up on his offer.

The rationale, behind the 90 day window, I learned later, was that most habits are created after 21 days of practicing a pattern of consistency; doing the same thing over and over and over again. Consequently, if I were to practice his teachings with consistency for 90 days without fail, I would be forming habits and uniformity in behavior that could produce nothing other than success.

I would develop an unconscious appetite for success and the discipline to work without effort. I would begin to activate, initiate and motivate my own success because the actions necessary to achieve it would become second nature, a part of my regular routine. I was convinced and decided to work with the 90 day gameplan. We sat down developed what I call my "life plan for success".

I had a strong desire to change my life and committed myself to working long hours after completing my obligations at my day job as a Systems Analyst. I had redefined what success meant to me and I was willing to learn, to improve myself and to copy my mentors, behaviors, attitudes and formulas in order to achieve it. I was very coachable and teachable. I had an open-mind. I wanted change and I was determined to get it.

The Sacrifice

My mentor and I started out on our 90-day journey and I did everything I was told to do, despite whether or not I agreed with it or felt like it. It was simple, but not easy.

First, I had to identify all of the bad habits I had been practicing for years. Next, I had to begin breaking these bad habits and replacing them with new, more productive, more challenging ones. These new habits I chose all had a purpose. Every new habit I was to develop had to contribute in some way whether large or small to the success I was seeking. Breaking old habits, however, was a little difficult for me.

Let me tell you, it is a distressing and difficult practice to break old habits. I had to do things I did not want to do and stop doing some of the things I enjoyed. The good news was that if I could form them in 21 days, I could surely break them in 21, well maybe 23.

I had to give up lounging around after work, looking at TV for hours, sitting around talking crap with my friends, hanging out after work and anything and everything that was non-productive for at the least 90 days.

I replaced those habits with activities that would help me to progress toward my goal and I can very vividly remember the many times my friends called me to go and hang out, and I had to decline.

Because they could not understand what was going on with me, friends and family alike took my declinations as negative. They called me names, began to suggest that I thought I was better than they and even suggested that I had forgotten from where I had come. In their eyes I had become a "Wannabe" …you know, "one who wants to be more than what he actually is". I was not taken seriously and no one believed I could do it.

While none of that was true, the negative peer pressure from my friends and the positive peer pressure from my mentor, sometimes made me feel as though my sanity was being crushed between two concrete pillars. My family thought that I was crazy. My girlfriend at the time was angry because I could not spend as much time as I had in the past shooting the breeze and wasting time. Even my father thought that I was sick and needed to get myself together. Everyone wanted to know if I had lost my mind. I was running morning, noon, and night. I worked early days and late, really, really late nights. Those 90 days felt like 90 years. I actually cried every morning on my way to work.

Because I appreciated my mentor's efforts to help me, I could not did not make any excuses. Excuses were unacceptable. I forced myself to produce and I made it happen.

Because I had obligations, I could not call in sick to work during those 90 days. I had to be committed to becoming a professional both in my job by day and my efforts to change my future by night. I tell you it was HARD.

My mentor, however, made the transition easier. He taught me to see the positive in everything I was doing, and he encouraged me every bit of the way. I read my assignments with consistency, attended meetings and trainings, acquired customers, made phone calls, took care of my son, went to work, and of course made tremendous progress.

He taught me to internalize the fact that progress was to be made everyday, not just on good days or the days or when I felt like it but *EVERYDAY*. After all, time is not something you can get back after it is wasted.

Through this experience, I earned a new respect for time. It became clear to me that time cannot be created, saved for a rainy day, or recreated. Time has its own agenda and we have to dance to its tune. As my father would say, "When the beat of the drum quickens, you have to change your steps; if not you ruin the rhythm."

At the end of my 90-day journey, I did not make my mark. Discouraged, however, I was not. I and my mentor simply set another goal and within ten days I met it.

What I set out to do in 90 days, I achieved in 100 days. The key here is that I did not give up. I quickened my steps, caught the rhythm and within 100 days, I had put myself in position to call the shots for my life.

The first shot I called - firing my boss of twelve years!

I have never worked another day in my life for someone else. I became my own boss, remain my own boss and continue to call the shots.

I tell you, it was the greatest challenge I have ever overcome and one of my greatest joys aside from the birth of my first son, Cory. The day I freed myself into a life that would allow me to do what I wanted was the most remarkable day of my life.

I practiced, and practiced, and practiced. I made progress, progress and even more progress. I became a professional networker and began to impact humankind. After all of the excitement began to wear, however, I realized that it would take an extraordinary amount of discipline to maintain my achievement.

Living The Five Wealth Principles LifePlan Consistency Strategies for Success ™

1. Make the decision to take daily action towards achieving your goals. Turn off the TV. Let the answering machine pick up your calls and begin doing the things that will contribute to your success daily. Sit down, focus and start making a list of at least ten (10) activities that are extremely pertinent to the success you desire. Start doing these things everyday. When you feel like and even when you don't. Only you can make success happen for you. I have not seen a farmer yet yield crop from a garden he did not cultivate with consistency. You determine the fruit which your tree will bear.

2. Define your short term goals. Do not put the pressure on yourself to attain success in 10 days. Be realistic. Sit down, really think through your overall long term goal and then break it up into sections that can be realistically attained in the short term. For example, if it is your desire to

learn to professionally decorate cakes. You can't start your pursuit of this knowledge with making the icing. You first have to master the fundamentals of baking a good cake worthy of being decorated. Let's put it another way, you can't pole jump your way into success. You have to get a running start.

3. HOLD YOURSELF ACCOUNTABLE. Don't wait for someone else to hold you accountable. Hold yourself accountable to your own actions every step of the way. Look at your actions objectively. In order of importance, make an If/Then table (see table 1, Appendix). If I do…then what?

4. Add to your progression with consistency. Once you accomplish a task, push yourself to do more and a little bit more and just a little bit more. Block out all negativity and keep moving forward. Digest those thoughts, attitudes, character traits and personalities of the successful people who influence your life. Tailor them to your specific needs and live.

5. Revisit your ultimate goal daily. Don't get off to a great start and then quit at the first hurdle. Keep moving. Prepare for the unexpected and remind yourself of the success you will achieve.

6. Remind yourself of the contribution your success will make to society. Jot down a list of at least twenty-five (25) positive impacts that your endeavors will have on you, your family, your friends, society and humankind all over the world.

7. Deliver on your promises. Be honest with yourself and others. Don't make promises to yourself or others that you cannot keep. Force yourself to become uniform in your behavior, especially when it comes to keeping your word. If you make a promise to yourself, for example, to finish a certain task, do it. Do not stop until it is completed. Exercising consistency establishes credibility. It builds character and more importantly, trust. You become a man or woman of your word and you establish loyalty among your colleagues.

8. Get out of your moral box! Step outside of your comfort zone. Explore new possibilities, new people, and new environments. Do not allow the words no, stop and don't continue to suppress your success. Start by telling yourself everyday upon rising, *"I can and I will succeed, I can and I will succeed...I CAN AND I WILL SUCCEED!*

9. Pray several times a day asking for strength, confidence, power, insight, clarity, vision, wisdom and creativity. The minute you get an idea that heightens your excitement, intrigues your interest and moves you to take action, go for it. Condition yourself to know that all things are possible. Take a minute to brainstorm some of the ideas or things you have wanted to explore but never had the guts to do it. Make a list, do some soul searching and start making things happen *EVERDAY*. Respond to Universe's demand to be the best that you can be and never let doubt or fear stand in your way.

10. Get rid of bad habits! Make a list of twenty (20) good habits and twenty (20) bad habits. Analyze each one of them and identify what motivates you to practice this habit. Continue to practice those good habits. Replace the bad habits as soon as possible with productive ones and never return to them. Reflect, regroup - revive.

11. Celebrate and treat yourself when a task/goal is accomplished or achieved. Do this in moderation. You do not have to celebrate every time you return a telephone call. Work hard so that you can play hard.

12. Fellowship with other high achievers. Take up a hobby or two that characterizes successful people. As you become more and more successful, you will find yourself in situations where - when in Rome, you have to do as the Romans do. Learn to play golf, or chess, racquetball, or even the history of fine wine. Equip yourself with the knowledge to participate in circles that are outside of your comfort zone.

DISCIPLINE

Effort without order equals chaos.

~ C. Anthony Harris

Before we get into the third wealth principle, let me say a bit about the title of this book Living the Five Wealth Principles.

Principles are defined as rules of conduct, fundamental laws, truths upon which others are based. The Five Wealth Principles are fundamental laws or truths, linked together, building upon each other to make solid foundations for success. Only when these five wealth principles are lived; developed as rules that govern your life and are practiced daily will they produce permanent and not temporal success.

As we learned in the previous chapters, to become successful you must pursue your goal with persistency on a consistent basis. In order to maintain that persistency and consistency, you must add discipline- an orderly conduct and system of rules to help govern your success daily.

Discipline will be the hardest, most difficult mountain you will have to climb on your journey. However, I guarantee, if you keep climbing higher and higher, everyday, you will reach the top.

DISCIPLINE

"The training or routine that improves skill" (dictionary.com).

Discipline is the most challenging of the five wealth principles because it requires you to develop the self-control to maintain a routine that contributes to your success daily, regardless of how difficult it may be. It requires you stay focused on your success, continue practicing the good habits you established in the last chapter and continue to refrain from the bad ones. Discipline requires you to obey rules whether you agree or disagree; to adhere to specific patterns of efficient behavior, develop the character to accept punishment intended for correction and make the necessary changes to behaviors you may have practiced most of your life.

Discipline has no respect for emotion. It sits at the core of your success and it operates as the foundation upon which the other principles build. For some, it will be the most difficult to master of all of the principles. Discipline is no joke.

The Test-Pass or Fail

How many times have you been tested to your breaking point or lost your "cool" when someone made you angry? 1...2...3? (when I get to your number just circle it) Why...self-control is not always easy.

How many times have you done just enough to get by? 1...2...3? Why...efficient behavior requires attention to detail and detail requires much more thought than mediocrity.

How many times have you broken the rules because you did not agree with them? 1...2...3? Why...submitting to a set of rules or authority, especially when you are in disagreement, goes against your personal desires and opinions.

How many times have you suffered harmful consequences because you failed to practice discipline? 1...2...3...50? Why...the result of disobedience to discipline is punishment and punishment hurts.

The point is, we have all been in situations where our level of discipline has been tested. Whether we passed or failed depends largely upon the discipline we used in response to the situation. This is why discipline is one of the most difficult of the five wealth principles to master.

Discipline requires us to perform on the spot. It requires us, in many cases, to do the total opposite to what we are accustomed. If you are a hothead, for example, and in the habit of giving people a piece of your mind, discipline will require you to keep quiet, diffuse the situation and move on. For some of us, that's not easy.

Oftentimes it is our emotions that get into the way of our logic and/or professionalism. When this happens we suffer consequences that could be detrimental to our success. So, let me offer a few words of caution.

Words of Caution

If you really want to be successful, it is extremely necessary to practice an enormous amount of discipline. Don't think for a minute that the day you "arrive" at success the tests are going to stop. That's only a myth. They actually get harder, more intense. People will continue to be the people they are and just because you are now experiencing success won't change them. How you respond to them in the face of adversity will. To avoid burning bridges you may have to cross again practice…that's right…discipline. You all are fast learners.

Mastering discipline is much like the game of darts. You have to put all of your efforts into hitting the target in the middle. While the other targets bring you closer to winning the game, hitting the bull's eye *guarantees* your win.

On your game board of life, imagine discipline as the bull's eye. Master this principle on your journey and you will win. Master discipline and all of the other wealth principles will fall right into place. You will automatically enhance your persistency, consistency, urgency and excitement. You will find yourself doing more, desiring less, making things happen and Living The Five Wealth Principles. Let's dive into the difficulty and get out quick.

The Difficulty with Discipline

Discipline is the most difficult principle to master, first, because it requires an immediate, mandatory change. It mandates the riddance of bad habits and demands the adoption of those that contribute to achieving your goals. This principle demands that you let go of some of the things you love and embrace those you may dislike.

Now, you were supposed to do this in the last chapter and begin practicing and developing your good habits. But, speaking from experience, I know it's easier said than done. So let's revisit from another angle. You've got to get those unwanted visitors (bad habits) out of the house and out of your life.

Cleaning House

When cleaning your house of those bad habits, get rid of them all. Don't get rid of the easily identifiable ones; the ones that are really messed up. Throw them all out! Even the ones you think don't have as much wear and tear as the others. You have to get rid of them all to make room for the new.

I personally had a hard time with this principle because I had to let go of habits that gave me pleasure. You know the ones we probably have in common like hanging out with the fellas, relaxing in front of the television, and, at times, doing absolutely nothing.

As I got deeper into my study of successful people, I discovered that these habits were not productive for my success. My mentors, I noticed, never seemed to take time-off. They worked consistently on developing new projects and improving old ones. Even when they seemed to be at "play", they were working.

After letting go of my bad habits and practicing the new, I actually began to enjoy myself. The fact that these habits were much more productive gave me an indication that I was on the right track. Meetings don't always take place in the boardroom. Some of the most meaningful business meetings occur on the golf course, over dinner, at the gym, at church, weddings, wine-tasting events, etc.

As much as I enjoyed the bad habits I had been practicing for years, they only added laziness, procrastination, and incompletion to my success and often created setbacks. The good habits, some I enjoyed and the others I learned to enjoy, pushed me forward in the direction of my success and it felt good.

    I met people who could teach me. I made friends with people who could assist me in my endeavors and keep me from making mistakes. More importantly, I met people who inspired me to do better.

    While working toward my goals, I made business deals, solidified partnerships and made friends sometimes all in the same meeting. The benefits were and continue to be awesome.

    I learned about real estate, mortgages, tax breaks, construction, advertising, you name it. And, I learned it all over coffee, breakfast, lunch, dinner, watching the game, playing golf and just shooting at the breeze. Trust me, although not easy, replacing bad with good is actually fun.

> When you can't find the rhyme, look for the reason. If you can't find the reason, accept it and move on.
>
> ~ D

Discipline is difficult, second, because it is a principle that has no respect for feelings or emotions. Sometimes there are things in life we must do even when we do not want or feel like doing them. Even when you don't understand the rhyme or the reason behind what you have to do, develop the discipline to do it anyway; especially if these tasks are beneficial to your success. Swallow your pride, disregard your feelings or emotions, practice discipline, continue moving toward your goal and don't be surprised when the necessity for discipline shows up.

Examples

All of us have encountered that boss, company policy, law or some form of leadership with which we disagreed. The only choices we had in these matters were to either follow the rules or break them. If we broke them, serious consequences were sure to follow. So, what did we do? Did we practice the necessary amount of discipline and follow the rules, regardless of how we felt? Or, did we fight a losing battle, go up in arms against them and still lose in the end?

Well, if you still have a job or you're not in jail, you probably mustered up the discipline to follow the rules. You may not have liked the feeling of submission at first, but the thought of losing your paycheck or your freedom, I confidently say, may have given you a pretty good incentive.

Sometimes the necessity for discipline shows when we are inconvenienced. This aspect of discipline is very difficult for some people, I don't know too many who love to be inconvenienced, myself included. Discipline, however, demands action on our part whether convenient or inconvenient; whether we like it or not. Remember that interview from hell? I am sure the majority of us have had at least one and the rest just aren't willing to admit it. So let's take a minute to set the stage.

You're traveling to a job interview and not quite sure where you are going. The original meeting place has been changed and what you thought was going to be a 20-minute straight shot, around the corner from your apartment turns into a 2-hour trip on a long winding, one-lane, dangerous road. What do you do? You need this job.

If you practice discipline, you deal with the inconvenience, prepare yourself the night before and get up at 4 am instead of 6. You do whatever it takes to make the journey and arrive at the interview on time.

Let's say you didn't practice discipline. You woke up late, printed the directions from Mapquest on your way out of the door, but you didn't follow them as written. You turned left when the directions said to turn right. You had to take that shortcut because you didn't prepare the night before and you're "running a little late". You got lost and eventually missed your appointment. You don't even have the job and you've missed work already?

Let's say you made it to the interview. Late, but nevertheless, you made it. In the eyes of the employer, you quite possibly have gone from strong candidate to irresponsible. The employer does not seriously consider you anymore because your actions don't prove that you take the opportunity seriously. You cause yourself financial hardship because you don't have an income and have now ruined your opportunity to get one. Ultimately, you've caused yourself even more of an inconvenience than if you had just exercised enough discipline to do what it took to get there on time.

You try to blame Mapquest, the traffic, your car, the line at the gas station but you can't. You can't blame anyone but yourself and your failure to practice discipline. You had the directions but you did not follow them. You were aware, well in advance, of what it would take to get there on time but you ignored it. You could have gotten gas the night before, but you didn't. You were busy celebrating the job you didn't get.

Don't make the same mistake with your chance at success. Get disciplined. Use the information in this book as your roadmap. Don't take a shortcut, skip to the end or just skim through. Take the time to learn these principles, internalize them and practice them daily. The more you travel a road, the more familiar it becomes, the shorter the distance, or so it seems. Your success is waiting on you. Don't be late.

Discipline and You

If you were a contestant on the Bachelor or the Bachelorette, I would strongly urge you to save the last rose for discipline and marry this principle. Your relationship with discipline is crucial. You must become intimate with it; when you do it serves as your secret place where you can always go for cover in the face of adversity. Trust me, you need discipline and an enormous amount of it.

Make no mistake about it. There will be times when you are told to do things or you are seeking the advice of leaders and you won't agree. You may even be insulted by the advice given, may feel like throwing in the towel and knocking out your boss. In certain situations you may even be right but don't lose your cool. When adversity comes, never lose sight of your confidence but don't let it get in your way either.

You have to remain in control of your emotions at all times. You may not agree with the advice or the task. Take it anyway, or just do whatever is asked (as long as it's legal that is). Remember, these are successful people who have already been where you are trying to go, whether you like them or what they have to say or not. Use their experiences to improve yours.

Bite your lip, stomp your toe, take a trip to the restroom to regroup if you have to but take the advice. You will have plenty of opportunity to sort it out later. Then, keep what you can use and throw the rest away.

Tin Cup

One of the greatest examples of the practicing discipline is portrayed by Kevin Costner in the movie Tin Cup. Costner plays "Roy McAvoy" in the movie, an amateur golfer on a journey to win the US Open. This guy has some experience with golf but is at a low in his life because he lacks discipline. Basically, he's a hothead who always let's his emotions get the best of him.

His caddy tries to tell him that his swing is off because he lacks the discipline to stay focused. The caddy gives him advice on how to improve his swing and threatens to leave if he doesn't follow it. McAvoy, at first questions his caddy but then decides to give in and take the advice.

Now, this was a breakthrough for McAvoy because throughout his life he never managed to master the art of accepting direction from others. As a result, he was never successful at anything and found himself always struggling to stay above water.

Because of McAvoy's stubbornness, it was very difficult for him to follow someone else's leadership. To make a long story short, McAvoy swallows his pride takes the advice and yes, improves his swing.

The point is, only when McAvoy decides to put down his strong will, ask for help and actually take the advice even though he disagrees and cannot see the logic in it, does his golf swing improve.

Your journey to success is no different than McAvoy's swing. It is not going to be easy. I would be lying to you if I promised that it would. It can, however, be *easier* than it has been in the past if you take the advice and the experience behind these principles and start living them. How much easier depends upon you and your commitment. The practice of discipline becomes easier and easier with practice. It does not ensure that obstacles won't get into your way but it will teach you how to handle them. It's not always the scientific solution that actually solves the problem, but how we respond to it.

Oh, No There's A Train On My Track!

Ever been on your way to an event and caught by a stalled train on the tracks? If you haven't, keep living, you will. If you have, what did you do? Did you decide to skip the event, turn around and go home or did you practice discipline and wait patiently for the train to pass? Did you choose a different route? Did you ever make it to the event?

If you did make it to the event, congratulations are in order. You practiced discipline and kept moving toward your mark regardless of the obstacle. What's important is not how you got there but *that* you got there.

Your journey to success requires of you this same discipline. If something gets into your way, don't let it stop you on your track. Patiently regroup and devise a plan to move it, find a way around it, over it, under it or through it. Never ever turn around, go home and quit. Develop the discipline to keep moving forward

What? There's More

Stay with me and pay attention. It gets better and better and better…just like the Energizer bunny. Let's keep going!

Don't Get Scared Now

Another difficulty with discipline worth mentioning is the difficulty we experience with doing things when we have no clue about the outcome. For most of us, it is extremely scary to put our time, money and energy into something without the guarantee that down the road we will see some benefit.

Many of us get scared when we venture out on this road less traveled. As soon as we discover there are no lights, no direction, no one else in sight, no gas station for miles and virtually no help if we had car trouble, we become reluctant to keep going. Our fear may overpower our desire to reach our destination and we may even consider traveling 100 miles out of the way to find "a safer road".

Let me warn you now. Your journey to success is going to take you through the mountains, down through valleys, through the busy cities and the lonely countryside. It will take you down some lonely, dark and desolate roads where there won't be another car in sight for miles. Don't get scared and turn around. Keep driving.

Fill up the cooler, visit the restroom, gas up and let's ride. You must keep going despite the fear your journey's road conditions presents. Face your fear. You have no choice. Develop the discipline to deal with it.

Facing Our Fear

Discipline forces success seekers to face fear. The trouble is fear wears many disguises. It can appear in our lives as a fear of rejection, a fear of disappointment, and more importantly, a fear of failure. It hides very cleverly in our excuses and the blame we place on others to cover our own inadequacies. If we are not careful to expose it, fear can steal our dreams, goals, ambition, drive, confidence, strength, power, persistency, consistency, discipline, urgency, excitement and our success. It usually goes a little something like this.

The Thief In The Night

We embark upon a journey toward success and hit the ground running. We are persistent. We know what we want and we go after it. We practice persistency. We accept the fact that success will not happen overnight and we prepare ourselves to develop uniformity in our behaviors and develop the consistency that will move us closer to our goal. In fact, we have become so consistent, our entire lives become consumed with nothing other than working towards our success. Copying successful people has become second nature and we are maintaining a strong positive progression toward our success. We're excited, motivated, bold, fearless and determined. Nothing can stop us. Until…

Until **FEAR** creeps its ugly head into our thoughts; until then, we were moving toward success like a freight train with no brakes. However, once we noticed the presence of fear, we immediately derail. We come to a screeching halt and stop all progress. We spend time trying to figure out where it came from but no time figuring out how to send it on its way.

While it is natural to be afraid in the presence of fear, it is not productive. You cannot allow fear to steal your desire for success. The only way to conquer it is to identify it, face it and develop the discipline to destroy it.

Now, you might be saying, "I'm not afraid, I know things won't be easy but I know what I'm doing." All of that may be true but, no matter how well things are going, at some point, fear will make a visit and it's usually unexpected. Trust me.

Your Date With Fear

Just as you prepared yourself for your journey by defining success for yourself, you have to prepare yourself for your date with fear in much the same way. You must identify the fear you are experiencing before you can deal with it. Some are not as bad looking as they seem. Let's take a look at the fear of rejection first.

The fear of rejection can be one of the most debilitating fears you will experience. When you present an idea, proposal, or even yourself to a person for whom you have great respect and high regard, your fear of rejection heightens. You know that you put your best foot forward but you begin to doubt, second-guess yourself.

You wonder if your product or business plan is professional enough to meet the person's expectations. If *you* are the presentation, you get your hair done, sit through a manicure and a pedicure, shave, get dressed in your Sunday best and worry all of the way to the door whether or not the person you are trying to impress will accept you. In both instances you are experiencing emotions that go along with the fear of rejection.

Let's say that your idea, your proposal or you were rejected. Whether you will admit it or not, your first thoughts will go toward self-degradation.

If your idea was rejected, you begin to doubt whether or not it was a good idea in the first place. You drop the project only to find someone else picked it up, ran with it and now they're on the cover of Fortune Magazine with "your idea".

You tell people, they stole your idea when, in actuality, all they did was pick it out of the dump *YOU* put it in. They cleaned it up and went after it with persistency, consistency, discipline, urgency and excitement. It's like my grandmother often said "one person's junk is always another's treasure", so be careful what you throw away out of fear.

If it was your business plan that was rejected, you begin to think that maybe it was not professional enough. You don't blame yourself. After all, you went to the local business association to get professional help. You get angry with the people who you hired to help and you place blame on them. You vow never to use their service again and because your proposal was rejected you, drop the entire project.

Lastly, if after all of your preparation, the person you are trying to impress rejects you, you don't take it lightly. Instead of accepting the fact that it just did not work out and moving on, you stereotype every woman or man that resembles this person in the slightest way and you avoid any and all possible relationships and even simple conversation. You see a well-dressed woman or man wearing the same color as this person did the night of your rejection and you never say two words to them. After all, they are all the same; if one rejected you, they all will reject you. Right? Wrong!

You could miss the opportunity to meet a great person, a potential friend, or maybe even a great business partner because of your fear of being rejected.

The Aftermath

If you're honest enough to admit that you have experienced these emotions, you understand how the fear of rejection can be debilitating. In each scenario, the project or object of desire was dropped and no success occurred.

The severity of the rejection increases depending on how badly you wanted whatever it was to work, how much time, effort and money you put into the project, how much faith you had in its validity and/or how much you admired the person of your attraction. As the severity of the rejection increases, so does its negative effect.

As the rejected person, you may become discouraged, feel unworthy, lose self-esteem, and may even become depressed. All of these emotions halt your progression towards your goal.

Depending upon how long you stay in this rut, you may never recover. You might try your hand at other ventures. Yes, you might design a new business plan or you may possibly approach another man or woman. However, in the aftermath of rejection, your efforts might be slightly superficial in the attempt to protect your feelings. Let me warn you. Taking the safe road may not always be the right road to success.

Don't allow the fear of rejection to destroy your drive to move forward. Face your fear. Deal with it and get over it. Understand that some things will work, some won't - so what... move on. SOMETHING WILL!

How Do I Trust That?

> Feared is the thing whose worth is unknown.
>
> ~ C. Anthony Harris

The experience with the fear of disappointment is more about the fear of the unknown than anything else. When we encounter this fear, many of us spend time entertaining the thought that there is no one we can trust. People are out to get us and ultimately, will, if we let their guards down.

We want to explore new ideas, new activities, and new people but we're so afraid we'll be disappointed we avoid the possibilities. We have the discipline to stick with the old tried and true. But, we can't bring ourselves to develop the discipline necessary for exploration of the new.

New and Improved

A few months back, I saw a TV commercial that illustrated the fear of disappointment perfectly. The commercial's focus is on a guy who has had the same car for over twenty years and the same car insurance for just as long. His sister had a pleasant experience with a company she would also like for him to try. She has a hard time getting him to switch companies, even though he would be saving money. Her brother would rather pay more than less because of his fear of being disappointed by a new company. He felt more comfortable sticking with what he knew instead of trusting the unknown-even if it meant saving money.

Many of us have been there. You know how we do it. We have less than a tank of gas left and 10 miles to empty. We pass by five gas stations but don't stop. We are in search of the one we know; the one we use all of the time as if our cars can really taste the difference and we are praying the whole time that we won't run out of gas before we get to *our* station.

Many of have also been on the other side of the fear of disappointment.

Sometimes the fear of disappointment causes us to take a risk with the *unknown* instead of developing the discipline to improve upon what we already know.

You want to start you own business, begin a new relationship, or even enter into a new business partnership. You know that in the past you have not had the discipline to complete anything you have started and you fear disappointing yourself and those that believe in you. Or, you have the discipline to complete the project but you're not quite sure if it will work the way you plan and you need help.

You have a business partner in mind that you trust to help, but he or she has not always been as responsible as you deem necessary. You know that this person is an asset but you fear they will disappoint you. As a result, you never ask them to join the business. You choose someone who has great credentials but no loyalty to you. They take you to the bank, and you lose-all because of your fear of disappointment.

Your fear of disappointment in this situation caused you to trust the unknown instead of practicing the discipline to improve upon that which you have had experience.

In both situations, your fear of disappointment overrides the control a little discipline could have provided and you lose.

Here's another scenario.

You meet someone who appears to be the perfect mate. I mean this could be the "one". You, however, have been disappointed in all of your past relationships. Consequently, you condition your mind to think that this one won't be any different than your past. Your parents divorced. Your grandparents divorced. All of your aunts and uncles have gone through divorce and you vow never to get married for fear of getting…that's right divorced. Out of your fear of disappointment, you anticipate things will go wrong.

In your relationships you begin to look at every little, irrelevant habit that turns you off in order to justify ending the relationship *before* you are actually disappointed. You refuse to really commit to the relationship and never to marriage because of your fear of disappointment. You end the relationship and could have missed a wonderful life with your soul mate.

Had you decided to develop the discipline to respond differently to your fears you might be living a fairytale life as we speak.

In every case presented, fear stops you from getting what you want.

> **Wise people don't willingly walk into a ditch.**
>
> ~ C. Anthony Harris

While the fears of rejection and disappointment can have an astounding effect on the discipline we practice on our way to success, the fear of failure has an even greater impact.

Many of us discipline ourselves and put our best foot forward as a result of the fear of failure. We don't want to look stupid or crazy so we rise to the occasion, even if it's temporary. This fear is evident in several aspects of our lives. Oftentimes the fear of failure causes us to settle for what is comfortable and avoid anything challenging. This type of fear is as dangerous as a double-edged sword.

The Double-edged Sword

On our jobs we perform to the best of our abilities as a result of the fear of failure. On the flipside, when a new position becomes available, we avoid applying because we are afraid to fail.

We know that the salary increase would be of great benefit but, we refuse the change because we are afraid we cannot learn the job or be effective in it. If we take the job and we are not effective, we revert back to the fear of losing the job. Consequently, we settle for the job that simply helps pay the bills. We don't want to "bite off more than we can chew". Instead, we become comfortable. We go crazy inside of our comfort zone but refuse to even attempt to get outside of it. We become paranoid about failure and we haven't even tried.

It is the fear of failure that can have you in a constant state of paranoia. If you are not careful it will control your every move. Discipline can help you conquer this fear but it has be a healthy discipline that you develop. Otherwise, you will ride an emotional roller-coaster until you do.

Discipline: Healthy vs. Unhealthy

Healthy discipline is the discipline you practice when you take a new job. You commit to learning what you have to learn in order to become successful at whatever it is you are doing. It is the type of discipline that adds to the success in your life. It is the discipline that keeps you moving toward the life you not only desire but also deserve.

Unhealthy discipline is the discipline you practice when you stay in a low paying job out of fear of your ability to rise to the occasion.

In the movie "Maid In Manhattan" Jennifer Lopez plays a character who is being encouraged by her peers to go after a management position. Out of fear, she does not apply. Lopez becomes the object of a Senator's affection and out of the fear that he will think less of her because she is a maid, she pretends to be someone she's not. She becomes very disciplined in playing the role of a rich woman, but failed to practice any discipline in trying to improve her own life through her own abilities.

Developing a discipline that is born out of the fear of failure will not get you closer to your success. What it will do is keep you from it.

What Will They Think?

Sometimes out of the fear failure, we worry about what others will think about us. We continue trying to keep up with the Jones' even when it's a struggle. It's ironic but we do it. Some of us actually develop the discipline to struggle so that we can look good in the face of others.

I have seen many people struggle to maintain an unrealistically huge mortgage just to keep their bragging rights about having the largest house on the block. They want to live in a certain neighborhood in an attempt to impress their families, their co-workers and friends. They buy fancy cars and rarely get to enjoy driving them because they can't afford the gas. These people actually get second and third jobs just to make ends meet. They struggle, they're stressed and ironically, they are, indeed, disciplined.

They have to be extremely disciplined to maintain three jobs. But are they truly successful or just overworked? If they have defined success for themselves as having a nice house, expensive cars, no time and a mountain full of debt, then maybe they are. If that's not how they define success, they're simply overworked, underpaid and undisciplined.

People who get themselves into situations for all of the wrong reasons are undisciplined. There is no other way to put it. They settle for situations that are not conducive to achieving true success. Think about it. What is "success" if you never have the time to enjoy it?

However you define success, there's one thing I know; it sure feels a whole lot better poolside in the backyard than it does in the graveyard shift employee's lounge.

Stop settling and start taking!

~ C. Anthony Harris

Because we fear the instability of the unknown, we settle for what life gives us instead of taking the risk to get what we really want. We become controlled by our fears and not our desires. I know. I am a living witness to the control fear can have over your life. The writing of this very book is my example.

Conquering Your Fear

I have had the thought to write this book for over 5 years now. For some reason or another I never got started. I tried to sugar coat my fear through the familiar 1, 2, 3's... I could have, I should have, and I would have. Looking back, I actually came up with some brilliant excuses.

I knew I had something to say; a message that could help people change their lives but I lacked the discipline to get past my fears-rejection, failure and disappointment.

You see, every time I had the thought to write, fear stopped me. My mind was boggled with questions like "What if people don't want to hear what I have to say? How do I convince people that living these principles will change their lives? How do I begin? Because I feared possible rejection, I never got started.

The thought would come to me again. And, again my mind would become boggled with questions. What if the book doesn't sell? How can I invest in something I don't even know how to do? I can't write. What if I can't put my thoughts on paper in a way where people understand them? What if I fail? I am a network marketer, not an author. Because I feared failure, I never got started.

The thought came to my mind yet again. And, again my mind was boggled with questions. What if I start and don't finish? What if something happens and things don't go the way they should? What if, what if, what if…? Because I feared disappointment, I never got started.

In retrospect, I know now that I was not disciplined enough to conquer my fear of failure. It is really important to understand what's going on here. Don't get me wrong. I was disciplined and I was good at facing my fears. But much like those bad habits I know you're still trying to sort, in hopes that you can keep a few, I was disciplined in the areas of my life that were comfortable.

You see, when I first began thinking about writing this book, I did so because I knew these principles worked. I practiced them daily. I lived them. They changed my life! These are the principles that guided me to the success I enjoy this very day. So why was I so afraid?

I was afraid because I had not conquered my fear of failure as well as I had thought. Oh, I did it when I first began with my mentor. That's how I began to think about and develop these principles into their current frameworks. I did it when I became an entrepreneur as well as when I became a success coach. Now, however, I was faced, with a task that I did not know how to do; a task that was way outside of my comfort zone.

You're probably thinking, how silly is he, he wrote the book. Why didn't he just practice the discipline he's teaching us about? And, you're absolutely right. As I am writing this, I am asking myself that very same question and the only proper response- my fear of failure.

I succumbed to my fear of failure. Even though I live these principles daily, I still suffer, at times, with a fear of failure. I share this with you because I want you to understand that even when you are living the five wealth principles, there will be times when you will need more of one principle than the other. You will continuously have to revisit the information in this book.

You will continuously have to improve your persistency, consistency, discipline, urgency and excitement. You have to practice these principles daily. Failing to do so opens an opportunity for you to slip. If you don't practice these principles daily, you open yourself up to making the same mistake I made-thinking I had mastered them to a point where I did not have to refresh.

Life's A Box Of Chocolates

Ok. I did not practice the discipline to conquer my fear of failure in the beginning. But, you're reading this book so congratulate me on my success in the end. Thank you, thank you, thank you. I appreciate that. Thank you. Ok let's get back to business so you don't make the same mistakes I did.

Instead of conquering my fear, I made excuses. I would convince myself that it wasn't the right time; that I had too many things on my plate; that I needed to take a break first and clear my mind and then I would start.

I told myself, "Well, I could start writing my book, if I knew how." I used the excuse that, "I would have started last year, but I have other priorities". I even tried this one, "I should have invested money into my book instead of that new set of expensive kites. But, what the hell, you only live once."

Every time I had the thought about writing my book, I was crippled by fear. I eventually became comfortable with not writing it because I sugar coated my fear with excuses.

I was afraid of the risk; afraid that people would not embrace my ideology; afraid that I would never finish, so why start.

Consequently, I did not do any research on what I thought I did not know about writing. I did not take any courses, nor did I ask for help. I did not devise a plan to schedule in the time to write. I found time to play golf, hang out, enjoy life, and to live full-time while working only part-time, but I never managed to find the time to write. I simply settled into my enjoyable life, ignored my desire to become an author and condoned my actions by convincing myself that I was already successful and life was as good as it could get.

Whenever there was something enjoyable I wanted to do, I did it, even when it had no contribution whatsoever to accomplishing my goal to become an author. I would tell myself: "Oh, what the fuss, you only live once." If I wanted it, I bought it. If there was a place I wanted to visit, I went. I was living *large*, but that small, quiet inner-voice haunted me daily.

I was having fun but I was disappointed with myself. I felt as though I had not accomplished enough in my lifetime. I felt like my life and its work had more of a purpose than I was actually fulfilling. I even seemed to find a new respect for Forest Gump. Life for me had become a box of chocolates, and I did not know which one I was going to get. I was simply eating away at life randomly and whatever the flavor of the day; it was cool with me. Pretty desperate, isn't it?

What it all really boiled down to was this. I was making moves that would enable me to afford the chocolates, but I had no real choice in the ones I was actually getting. I was living a prepackaged life, finely packaged according to my financial status, but void of my own personal and emotional desires. My "moral box" had gone from hard-working 9 to 5 laborer, to young, daring and successful, but never fulfilled. Then came the day when I got that one chocolate that changed my whole outlook on the rest of the goodies that were in my life's box.

My Day Of Reckoning

As I remember it, I mentioned to a friend my desire to write a book. The thought came and went. The same day, my inspiration for this work and now my editor and I were talking. We engaged in a very pleasant discussion about spirituality and the recognition of pure and sincere hearts. We discovered that we had a lot in common. Unbeknownst to me, Angel overheard my conversation about writing a book.

One day while shooting the breeze, Angel expressed an interest in opening a business. My response was "So why don't you?"
 She did not respond right away. When she did, the question posed to me hit me like a ton of bricks. Angel asked, "If it's really that simple, why haven't taken your own advice? Why haven't you started writing your book?"
 I was speechless! How did she even know I wanted to write a book? I never talked to her about that.
 Astounded as I was, I regained my composure and we continued to talk. The second blow came when Angel began to remind me about just how precious time was and how it waits on no one. She went on to talk about making the best of the life we have, taking advantage of the opportunity, seizing the moment, how life was not a dress rehearsal but a "live act." Wow, I thought.
 I didn't know how to respond so I began with my excuses. Well, I woulda…, I began. Cut off at the pass, Angel interrupted and mocked me.
 "Coulda, woulda, shoulda, bottomline…you didn't," she said.

At first I got angry; not with Angel, but with myself. Nothing said was untrue. I was angry because I was being forced to identify and ultimately deal with the fear that had controlled me for the past five years and I was not ready.

I asked myself "Why *have* I spent so much time wanting to write a book and not writing it?" It was a bitter-sweet moment. For the past five years I had been training others to change their lives through living these principles and failed to train myself. Having the tables turned, if you will, forced me to meet the fear that had kept me from achieving the one goal I had a burning desire to accomplish and this time I couldn't find an excuse good enough to avoid it.

Through training someone else, I was being forced to deal with same fear I warned others about; see, I told you it works.

Thanks for reading my book. Keep going, there's even more good stuff on the way.

You Are More Than A Conqueror

You might be experiencing the fear of rejection, the fear of failure or the fear of disappointment in this very moment. Again, some things will work, some won't, so what…SOMETHING WILL the moment you develop the discipline to make it happen. Approach your success from different angles. Improve the areas of weakness. Strengthen your strengths. Pick yourself up. Dust yourself off and try, try, try again. NOTHING BEATS A FAILURE BUT A TRY! I did it and you can too!

    Move through fear the same way you move through life. Discipline your mind to focus on possibilities and not pitfalls. Stop being afraid of the unknown. When you embark upon a venture, you don't know what pitfalls will hinder your progress. You don't know if everything will work according to your plan. You don't know if all of the time, effort, money and faith you put into the project will make a profit or not. But, in order to be successful you have to try. You are more than a conqueror.

The Millionaire Myth

    Over the last few years, I have come in contact with thousands of people who believe the myth that to build a successful company, you must have thousands and thousands or maybe even millions of dollars before you even begin. Absolutely not true. What you have to have is a vision, a level of persistency, consistency and an enormous amount of discipline. Take a look at the story behind Mike Domek.

Mike Domek

In 1992 Mike Domek ran out of money for college. Instead of accepting the hand that life had dealt, he decided to try selling tickets to events to help with the cost of his education. He started his business in a one-bedroom apartment with $100 dollars and, that's right you've got it- DISCIPLINE.

For seven years Domek disciplined himself to work at building his business and keeping his profits in-house. He was persistent and consistent. While he never made it back to college, over the years he built strong business relationships with ticket brokers across the country.

Today, Domek's business has grown from a one-bedroom apartment, no employees and no profit, to a 1,600 square foot building with seven employees and some profit, to a 16,500 square foot office space with 170 employees and over $120 million in sales in 2005.

How does a college drop-out, with no money, no employees, and no fancy office in downtown Manhattan do it?
DISCIPLINE!

Mike Domek, pursued his dream with a discipline that forced him to work early mornings and late nights. He worked during holidays; through weekends; and while his friends were hanging out. Despite the odds that were stacked against him, he did not give up. He continued to work at making his dreams come true and today enjoys the fruits of his labor.

To get where you want to be in life and not where life puts you, you have to start focusing on what you want and not what you don't have or wish you could get. You then have to do what it takes to get there. Without this type discipline you will forever focus on your negatives and never give any attention to your positives. Think about it?

How would you have dealt with the embarrassment of having to leave school? How would you have dealt with the disappointment? What would have been your alternative?

By His Grace

The Domek story really hits home with me because I too have had to answer these questions. I was forced to drop out of school because I had a son to support. I had to work in order to care for him and I, too, had hopes or returning and never did.

I, like Mike, had to deal with disappointing my parents. I did not have a clue as to how I would provide for my family; all I knew was that I had to do it. I had to work. I had to work when I felt like it and when I did not. I had to work jobs I liked and a few I disliked; bottom line, folks, I had to develop the discipline to work no matter what the circumstances surrounding me.

Domek is a success story we can all relate to because we also have to come up with working plans to survive everyday. We have to develop the discipline to work our plans like Domek did and continue to find ways to make the plan work for us.

When we look at the slow progression of Domek's business, we should be encouraged. I included Mike's story because I want you to understand that you don't have to have lots of money to become successful.

You develop the discipline to work with what you have and continue to build from there. As you build, you make sacrifices both small and large and you keep building.

When you begin to practice the wealth principle of discipline, you will strengthen your will power, you will develop a winning spirit and you will become unstoppable.

Living The Five Wealth Principles LifePlan Discipline Strategies for Success ™

1. Develop discipline with persistency and consistency. Work at it everyday without ceasing. Practice all three of these principles interactively in everything that you do.

2. Make a list of 12 bad habits you have to get rid of and 24 good habits that will contribute to your success.

3. Make a commitment to yourself to drop at least 1 bad habit and adopt 2 productive habits each month. If you can drop more than one bad habit great, but focus on one and really get rid of it before you work on another.

4. Practice the productive habits you have picked up DAILY until they become second nature. Once you have mastered your list, create another and another and another. Pretty soon, everything you do will benefit your journey to success.

5. Think about all of the projects you have wanted to start and didn't. Choose the one that is most important to you and BEGIN. Start by going to the nearest library or to the internet. Research as much information as you need to make a new and intelligent start at your future.

6. Create a list of 10 fears that have stopped you from pursuing your life's dreams. Explain why and how these fears have slowed down or stopped your progression toward success. Read and re-read your responses and say goodbye to these fears. Take that list, ball it up, burn it, throw it away, flush it…whatever. Identify, analyze and get rid of the fear that has kept you standing in your own way.

7. Make a list of at least 4-5 major tasks in relation to your project that you would like to complete by the end of the month. Get a calendar. Hang it on the wall, the refrigerator or some spot where it is clearly visible. Choose your deadline dates and work at completing each task before moving

on to the next. Do not over-extend yourself. Be reasonable. You cannot complete your life's work within a month.

8. Never make excuses for not practicing discipline. Instead, discipline yourself to do better and/or accept the consequences of your lack thereof. Choose an area in your life where you know your discipline is weak. Decide on one or two relevant activities and make a promise to yourself to do them daily. This strategy will help to sharpen your skill in discipline and allow you take more responsibility in getting things done.

9. Decide on how much time per day, per week, per month you will spend working towards achieving your goals. You might decide to commit to working 2 hours everyday or 3 hours once a week, whatever your preference, make time to work on your success and increase it, gradually. Don't overwhelm yourself. Be reasonable.

10. Confide in a trusted friend or mentor about the changes in your life you have decided to make. Ask them to help keep you focused and accountable. Challenge each other to meet deadlines and meet them!

11. Practice discipline and become a person of your word. Discipline, if practiced daily, sharpens your integrity, your trustworthiness and your reliability. If you say you are going to show up at 2:00 pm, show up at 2:00 pm and be punctual. Return calls, emails, respond to letters, questions and concerns, immediately, not two or three months after you get them. Commit to keeping your word whether it is with yourself or others. This discipline earns respect. People love most those who they can depend upon.

12. Do not stand in your own way. Know that you can do whatever you put your mind to. When you don't know something, ask, research, find the answers to your questions or but never, ever get discouraged and quit.

You are well on your way to the success you desire and deserve! But let's not have the party too prematurely. There two additional principles you need to master-urgency and excitement. These last two principles will put the icing on the cake. They will jumpstart your journey to success and send you on your way to a life where you are not only Living The Five Wealth Principles, but you are also enjoying the benefits it brings. Congratulations on the wealth and success you now experience-spiritually, mentally, physically, professionally and financially. Keep reading.

URGENCY

Beyond your circumstance your success exists.

~ C. Anthony Harris

So many times we fail to achieve success in pursuing our goals because we have gotten into the bad habit of procrastinating. We are waiting for the right time, the right place, the right person and/or the perfect circumstance. The sad news is that right time, that right place, person or the perfect circumstance, either comes too late or never at all. Deep down inside we know we can't blame anyone or anything other than our lack of urgency for our failures. We become angry and discouraged and often resort to doing nothing. All hope, however is not lost. Practicing the principle of urgency will help you get rid of your habits to procrastinate.

    It's your fault that you didn't develop a mindset for success and open the coffee shop down the street before Starbuck's took your spot. It's your fault that you did not move fast enough on that big real estate deal and now someone else is living in your dream home. It's your fault that you did not call the employer back until two weeks after the interview and the job was given to someone else. It's your fault that you put off until tomorrow the things you should have done today and the coupon expired. It's your fault you never practiced urgency and now have to suffer major consequences. And, it will be your fault if you don't spend the time and energy to change.

If you are a procrastinator, this chapter is definitely for you. While procrastination can damage your success, practicing urgency can repair it.

Urgency is the principle that reminds us time waits for no one. It is the principle that warns "if you don't get urgent about your business you will be up a creek with no paddle '…for night come when no man can work' (John 9:4)". Urgency is the principle that forces us to appreciate and not waste the time we have and it is the principle that can help you to see rapid changes in your level of success.

Now, you might be thinking that you are on track and nothing can stop you now. Well, if you have defined your success and you are working towards it through the practice of persistency, consistency and discipline, you are on the right track. Add a sense of urgency to your routine and you will stay on track and keep moving forward.

Stop, Drop and Roll

As I write this chapter I am reminded of a woman who was extremely successful and suddenly, without warning, her life went up in flames.

After being married for over 30 years and building a successful business with her husband, she enjoyed life in a half of a million dollar home and drove the finest of cars. She put everything she had into building and maintaining their success including her faith that they would continue this way forever. She, never took the time, nor did she feel the need to pursue any of the passions she desired personally. Unselfishly she focused her goals on the success that was good for the family.

One day, with no warning, her husband announced he wanted a divorce.

Well into her senior years, she found herself at rock's bottom-no job, no degree, no work experience, no money and no way to get any. Her husband had set fire to the middle of her life and her only option was to stop, drop and roll with the punches.

Unfortunately, I do not know how her story ends, but I can only imagine the panic, the nervousness, and the confusion she felt about what to do and how to start over. While she should have been planning for retirement, she now had to develop an immediate plan for survival. She had to practice urgency in getting her life back on track.

Urgency: By Definition

By definition, urgency is the motive or reason to impress or impel to some immediate course of action or activity. The woman's story exemplifies this and although unfortunate, it is not uncommon. Millions of people all over the world are forced to practice urgency whether they are prepared or not.

Urgency may be necessary because they lost their job and have to find another to avoid being evicted by the end of the week. Maybe a loved one died or becomes ill and they are left alone to provide for themselves. Maybe, it's your senior year and your graduation depends on the score of one last assignment you have to complete by the end of the day. Whatever the situation the practice of urgency is required to create the circumstance you desire.

Create Your Circumstance

> **Stop waiting on the perfect circumstance. It's not coming!**

If you truly want success and are serious about changing the way you live you have to stop waiting on the perfect circumstance and start creating it. Stop getting caught up in the when's…when I get a new car; when I get a new job; when I lose weight; when I get my finances together; when I; when I; when I. By the time you *actually do* it's a new year and you are in the same position you were last year. Break the cycle!

This will be a little more difficult for those of you who have managed to master the art of procrastination. Urgency may not be appealing. But, if you want different, you must do different. You do not have all of the time in the world to wait on the perfect circumstance. It's not coming. Just when you think that perfect circumstance is ringing your doorbell, you open the door only to find your ex and I guarantee, the time you spend trying to get rid of it could have surely been better spent. Use the time you have wisely. Stop waiting to create the circumstance you want for your life. The time is now!

If you want to become an entrepreneur, spend your time researching how to start your own business instead of sleeping eight hours per day.

If you want to lose weight, spend time in the gym exercising instead of on the couch watching infomercials on TV and maybe even ordering two of the latest weight lost gadgets just in case you misplace the one you will never use.

If you want to experience wealth and success-spiritually, mentally, physically, professionally and financially start living the five wealth principles outlined in this book instead of just taking notes.

Urgency And You

I cannot stress enough the importance of you developing urgency and practicing it daily with everything you do. Time, people, is not a toy. You have to assume the responsibility for your future and seize the opportunity to make it the best.

Understand that what you do today determines how you live tomorrow. When you open your mind to making the proper sacrifices now the destination to success will be that much shorter. It may not happen overnight but it will happen. Look at Howard Schultz.

Howard Schultz

If you are not familiar with Howard Schultz I am positive you are familiar with his coffee. Schultz is the mastermind behind Starbucks. What began as a mere thought has now become an international phenomenon and has become a household name. It didn't happen overnight, but it happened.

Howard Schultz began working on his dream over 13 years ago. It took him thirteen years to establish only five stores. Despite the obstacles, setbacks and whatever circumstances surrounded his life at the time, he did not quit. Understanding the power behind preparation, Schultz used his time wisely. He continued working towards his success and what took him 13 years to do in the past, now happens in one day. On average, Schultz opens five Starbucks stores per day and has over 12,000 worldwide.

When You Don't, Someone Will

    In my profession as a network marketer I have tried for years to force my partners into the practice of urgency. Time after time after time I would encourage them not to procrastinate, to take the bull by the horns and go after the success they envisioned for themselves right away. I kicked, screamed and hollered but to no avail. They did not seem to budge until the fear of loss showed up.
    In this industry, success is a numbers game. Whoever gets the most customers, in

the least time wins. Consequently, logic suggests, my partners would be working feverishly the entire quarter to increase their customer base and not the night before the winners were to be announced. Not so. For some reason they seemed to think that their immediate need get a customer point in the system was their potential customer's urgent concern.

Many of my partners would slack off until the final week of competition. Oh, they would attempt to make contacts but sometimes failed to followed-up. Not until someone else acquired that one last customer they needed in order to make bonus did they see the necessity of urgency.

You see, what my partners did not understand was that time was not going to stop and wait for them to get more customers. It was going to keep ticking away whether they were using it productively or not. So, I caution you- appreciate time and respect its power; when you don't, there's always someone else who will; that's the person who wins.

Time Is Of The Essence

The desire for success, like anything else, begins with a thought. To become a reality, it must move from thought to action and it must move quickly. Contrary to what some of us believe, we do not have all of the time in the world. Time is of the essence. The day I really comprehended this, is the day I began writing this book.

As I explained earlier, for five years, I *thought* about writing a book. I said I would but I didn't. I would forget about it and then the thought would come again. Until I actually sat down and began to write-my book was only a thought and what good is a thought if it is not shared?

At times, I wonder where I'd be today if I had written this book five years ago. How many people would I have helped? How would my life be different? How much sooner would I have arrived at the success I enjoy if I had been living my life and pursuing my goals with persistency, consistency, discipline, urgency and excitement?

Think about the thoughts you have let slip away from the light of day into the darkness of your mind. How many of your great ideas have you seen others bring to reality and experience the success you feel you deserve? How many times have you said, "I'm gonna…tomorrow," and tomorrow never came? How many times have you let regret, cripple your future? How many times have you failed to practice urgency?

Time-It's Priceless

In April of 2005, my Dad fell deathly ill. I was away on business and traveling to a conference I had been organizing for months. When I got the call to come home and the plea for urgency was made, I did not hesitate. I stopped everything I was doing and made the necessary arrangements to get home ASAP. I did not think about the cost, the event I would have to miss, or anything other than getting home to be with my Dad.

What I would lose financially, I knew I would gain spiritually; priceless precious

Time can neither be bought nor sold only respected!

~ C. Anthony Harris

memories. I had no choice other than to allow urgency to control my every move. My only concern was taking advantage of the moments I had left to talk with my Dad, express my love to him and just hold him before losing the opportunity forever.

By God's grace I made it and was afforded the opportunity to spend the last two days of my Dad's life by his side.

I share this story because too often I witness people dealing with unnecessary regret. For whatever reason they have allowed procrastination to replace their sense of urgency and they have suffered as a result.

Whatever your reason, when you procrastinate and do not take the time to pursue the things that are important to you, you stand the chance of losing them forever.

You cannot relive the events of yesterday, nor can you change them. It is what it was and it (time) keeps moving forward according to its own agenda not yours or mine. With every tick we are a second away from yesterday and a second closer to tomorrow.

Will you use it wisely, or will you watch it pass like a ship in the night? Remember, your success is not going to drop from the sky. You have to make the decision and then put the time into making it happen.

Ninety percent (90%) of my success came because I developed a sense of urgency about changing my life's circumstance. I was urgent and determined. As I mentioned earlier, I had only 90 days to change a circumstance I had lived for 17 years. When you do the numbers, that's 5,840 days, weeks, months and 46,720 hours of doing things outside of my true desires; all time I can never get back.

At first I thought what a waste. But, as I began to live the five wealth principles I began to understand, that the only way for me to know where I wanted to go, was to see where I had been.

My experiences showed me I did not want to punch a time clock for the rest of my life. I was able to see clearly that life for me meant working part-time, living full-time and helping others.

Had I not decided at that very moment in time to change my life through living the five wealth principles, I might still be somewhere *talking about wanting* to write a book. I thought it, I said it and I did it.

What is it that you have thought of, but not taken the time to do?

Word to the wise…if you think it, do it. If you don't take advantage of the time you have, it may never come again. Tomorrow will come, no matter what it brings with it. Don't let it come with a truckload of regret.

If there be no success, let it not be for the things you did not take the time to do; the dreams you refused to bring to reality, the goals you did not work at achieving, or the journey to success you failed to travel. Get urgent! Live every day as if it were your last and start building brighter futures for yourself and your families. Take what you want from life and under no circumstance settle for what it gives. I did and you can too! Excited? Good. Let's move on.

Living The Five Wealth Principles LifePlan Urgency Strategies for Success ™

1. Give thanks and praises everyday, for time is promised to no one.

2. List five examples of situations that where you were forced to practice urgency. Think about how you felt when the situation occurred, how you handled it and how you felt afterward.

3. Create a to-do-list and give yourself timeframes within which you must complete each task. i.e. If your to do list includes cleaning the kitchen, give yourself 15 minutes to wash the dishes; 20 minutes to clean the refrigerator, 5 minutes to sweep the floor and 10 minutes to mop. Be sure to stay within each timeframe.

4. Reflect on your feelings while using urgency strategy #3. Think about how you felt. Were you more or less determined to complete the tasks as the time ran out?

5. Realize that time waits for no one. It sticks to its agenda whether we agree with it or not. Take some time and sit in a quiet room with a clock. No matter what is going on around you, the clock keeps on moving, tick by tick. The batteries may run out in your clock but that still does not stop time; it's still moving. Stop procrastinating!

6. List five procrastinations you find yourself doing consistently. Make the decision to change and do it.

7. Make an assessment of how you are currently using your time. Write down ten of your daily tasks and take note of how long it takes you to complete each one.

8. After you have assessed the way you use your time. Commit to trimming at

least 6 minutes from each task. You have now freed an hour in your day to do something else.

9. Dare to dream. Think of five experiences you would like to have with your family and friends. Prioritize your list and do them. If you think it, do it. Don't wait.

10. Organize your day. Create a schedule and stick to it. If you have errands to run, do so in an orderly fashion. Don't travel to the other side of town to save 10 cents. The time and money you spend burning gas is not worth the trip.

11. Stop wasting time getting ready to get ready to start a project. Make a move, and get started. While you are planning to live, life is being lived.

12. Set deadlines and make sure you meet them. When you do, celebrate your success with some small reward. When you do not meet your deadline, take away something you enjoy, but never ever make excuses.

EXCITEMENT

Your excitement attracts the masses, your grumbling warns.

~African Proverb

Hoorah!!! You are well on your way to developing a mind, body, soul and way of life that is productive to your success! EXCITED? You should be!

Excitement is the energy that will keep you going. As I have mentioned before, all five of the wealth principles described in this book work together. They feed off of each other's energy. If you are excited about a specific goal or task, you will have no problem employing persistency, consistency, discipline, or urgency. Once you achieve that goal or complete that task, successfully, you will be so excited about your accomplishment you will have the drive to do more and more and more. Your life will become synonymous with SUCCESS!

Excitement: By Definition

Excitement is the wealth principle that calls us to a higher energy level and arouses us to action. When you become excited you exert a positive energy that makes you feel as though you can conquer the world. You are happy, you feel good about yourself and you have fun. When you are experiencing excitement about the goals you are accomplishing in life, no one has to coach you to success. You are on the home stretch and nothing and no one can stop you. You, don't have to be encouraged to start, continue or complete a task. You are aroused to action and you are enjoying it. More importantly, when you are experiencing excitement you practice persistency, consistency, discipline, and urgency and get things done. I know I experienced it.

When I actually put pen to paper and began writing this book, I was so excited I could not stop. I found myself writing in the wee hours of the morning and the late hours of the night. When I did not have pen and paper, I wrote inside my head, in the shower, during meetings, while listening to my mentors. I was so excited, I could not wait to get back my office, or any place, for that matter, where I could write my thoughts down. I wrote on napkins, business cards, magazines, whatever was available at the time, so as not to forget my thoughts. I lived and breathed Living The Five Wealth Principles and I was proud. I had finally gone from thought to action it seems in 0.1

seconds. Ok. It was five years, but whose counting. Don't ruin my excitement.

Once I began bringing my lifelong dreams out of the darkness in my head and into the light of reality, my excitement drove me to become persistent, consistent, disciplined and urgent about the completion of this book. Living the Five Wealth Principles consumed my thoughts, my actions, and my very existence. This project was my breakthrough. What will be yours?

I want you to think back for moment and reminisce on how good excitement feels. Can't quite get there on your own, well let me help.

Excitement And You

Remember the feeling that came over you just before your wedding day, your first day on the job, the birth of your son, daughter, grandson, granddaughter, niece or nephew? Remember how your heart raced when you opened the door to your first home or got the keys to your first car? Remember your first A in class or the first time you made the honor roll? Remember your first boyfriend, your first kiss?

Remember how you couldn't sleep the night before graduation, or better yet, the night before retirement? Well, let me tell you all of the emotions, anxiety, nervousness, eagerness, and anticipation you felt when you experienced one or more of these events are examples of excitement and it is this type of excitement that keeps you moving toward achieving success. You will be ready to conquer the world. But, let me warn you, it cannot be done in one day.

Rome Wasn't Built In A Day

Because excitement is an emotion that we can create for ourselves, it is extremely powerful. It has the power to drive us forward, but can also have the power to keep us standing still. I'll use myself as an example.

Again, in my experience with writing this book and developing the training materials for Living the Five Wealth Principles, I was so excited; the ideas were popping off of my forehead like sweat. I was so excited; I wanted to do everything right away.

I was fortunate to have a partner who encouraged me to "slow down". That was the best advice I could have gotten. Had I not slowed down, I would have crashed into success instead of coasting into it. Trust me, you prefer to coast. It feels a lot better.

When we get excited, we tend to take action right away. Many of us don't take the time to think things through. We don't weigh the pro's and con's. Ultimately, we put the buggy before the horse and wonder why we aren't moving.

Don't let your excitement get out of control. If you do, the project will appear larger than life. You will be so excited you won't know where to begin. If you aren't careful you'll retreat, thinking, there is no way, I can get it all done. Unless…that's right…unless you are truly practicing and Living The Five Wealth Principles.

If you are excited because you have practiced persistency, consistency, discipline, urgency to get you to where you are on your journey to success, by all means I congratulate you. You have obviously defined success and mapped out a plan to get there.

Maintain your excitement, but don't go too fast too soon. Do not make the mistake of putting on too much pressure to get things done in a hurry. This type of haste could cause you to make serious and maybe even expensive mistakes.

Going too fast too soon will have your mind all over the place. Continuing like this with no direction will only put you back to where you started at the beginning of this book. This haste will put a dent in your persistency, consistency and the discipline you need to stay focused and get things done. You will find yourself blowing out your birthday candles before you even bake the cake. Then, you'll begin to procrastinate, lose your sense of urgency and have to start all over again. After all of your hard work, how can anyone get excited about that?

Take caution, slow down, maintain and continue using the four wealth principles that got you to the point of excitement. If for some reason you are not excited yet, analyze the situation.

If you have reached the last leg of your journey and you are not excited, something is wrong. Reflect and regroup. The problem may be that you worked hard at using these principles for the wrong reasons. You may, for example, have gotten married to the wrong person. Athough you had a gut feeling it would not work, you did it anyway; your birthday is next week, you've only known this person for a couple of days, but it's in your life's plan to have that accomplished by age 29. You may have had a baby just so you could experience changing diapers, cuddling, and cooing but, you made no preparation for the challenges of parenting or the lifetime commitment. You may have graduated college or worked jobs you didn't like just to impress others. You may have made the mistake of becoming persistent, consistent, disciplined and urgent for everyone's excitement but your own. No worries, you haven't done anything wrong. You just need to regroup.

    You have made tremendous improvements in the way you live. Continue to apply and develop these principles into every aspect of your life, practice them daily and grow into a way of life with the power to create the circumstance you desire. Complete the journey. Begin a new task. Accept a new challenge and be sure you're doing so to please you.

    As I have said earlier, excitement is an easy principle to master because you can control it. Get excited and find pleasure in being happy, hopeful, creative, positive, productive, *persistent, consistent, disciplined and urgent.* Create in you a winning spirit and commit to winning. If you want more excitement, create it. Surround yourself with exciting people. Visualize the completion of your project. See your success. Focus on your future and stay excited. Don't sweat the setbacks celebrate the successes. Reward yourself and more importantly, hype yourself up-it's your match and you are the prize fighter.

  Don King has never entered the ring as a fighter, thrown a punch or taken a hit. He is, however, more excited about a fight he is promoting than the fighter himself. King's excitement incites excitement in spectators all over the world. People travel from near and far and spend millions because they feed off of the excitement produced by Don King. I encourage you to do the same. Making excitement a part of your life, draws people to you. It helps you to have fun on your journey and enjoy YOUR SUCCESS!

Living The Five Wealth Principles LifePlan Excitement Strategies for Success ™

1. Celebrate small successes. Set time limits and deadlines for completing tasks and complete them. Take notice of your level of determination and excitement about finishing project as you near the end of the allotted time.

2. Identify five successful/famous people whose excitement you admire and think about why. Rip off and duplicate what you like about their personalities and incorporate these things into your own.

3. Affirm and declare DAILY in front of your mirror "I am excited!" Really mean it and get excited about your excitement!

4. Practice seeing the brighter side of every situation. Be the life of the party. Excitement draws people to you.

5. Continue to be excited about who you are and the person you will become as you begin to create the circumstances *you* desire. Step into your greatness.

6. If you are calm, cool and collected or bubbling over with excitement, there is always room for more excitement. Take it up a notch. Put that excitement on autopilot! Increase your level of excitement by at least 50%. Let go, let loose and have fun. Pay attention to how much more productive you are when your happy.

7. Surround yourself with five exciting productive and successful people you know.

8. Go out and meet (I did not say marry) at least three (3) new people everyday.

9. Think of something you've wanted to do but never have. Get excited and do it. Write down the feeling you had before and after and continue to create that excitement in whatever you do.

10. Become a kid again. HAVE FUN!!!! Don't become immature, but enjoy life and get excited today!

11. Reflect on five (5) activities that excite you. Identify why these things excite you and find ways to apply these activities in other areas of your life.

12. Become that beacon of light for your family, your friends, your co-workers, and your acquaintances. Become the person everyone remembers, wants to spend time with and admires. The energy you give is the energy you receive.

CONCLUSION

Opened eyes don't continue to travel blind.

~*Author Unknown*

CONGRATULATIONS! You have are now empowered with a way of living that will help you complete your journey to success, bring your dreams into reality and create the circumstance you desire.

Continue to follow this roadmap and share it with as many people as you can. Help someone else see the value of Living The Five Wealth Principles and show them the way to enjoying wealth and success- spiritually, mentally, physically, professionally and financially. Life will always be a trip, so you might as well take the ride and turn it into a vacation.

Sometimes you will need to practice more discipline than you will persistency. Other times you will need more excitement to help you with consistency. You might need to be a little more urgency with getting things done. Find your balance. Whichever principle you need the most of at any particular time, practice it. Not only do these principles work together with each other, they also work together with you.

I wish you all the best and encourage you to attend my trainings as often as possible. Use this book as a reference. Read it again and again and again. Continue to stay focused, and remain inspired. Enjoy your success. Begin living full-time and working part-time. Be proud of yourself and use the knowledge, strength and power to live a healthy, happy, safe and successful life. Let your story be an inspiration to someone else. Live, love, laugh and I will see you on the beaches of the world.

APPENDIX

Live, laugh love and enjoy wealth and success-spiritually, mentally, physically, professionally and financially!

~ C. Anthony Harris

Table 1.   If I…then what?

If I…	Then
If I practice living the five wealth principles…	My journey to success will go smoother.

Living The Five Wealth Principles LifePlan for Success Journal ™

Living The Five Wealth Principles is a way of life. To develop the lifestyle of success you not only desire but deserve, you must incorporate these principles into your daily routine and practice them seriously. Use the LFWP LifePlan Success Journal to chart and evaluate your progress.

LFWP LifePlan For Success Journal™

Persistency

LFWP LifePlan For Success Journal™

Consistency

LFWP LifePlan For Success Journal™

Discipline

LFWP LifePlan For Success Journal™

Urgency

_____
_____
_____
_____
_____
_____
_____
_____
_____
_____
_____
_____
_____
_____
_____
_____
_____

LFWP LifePlan For Success Journal™

Excitement

LFWP LifePlan For Success Journal™

LFWP LifePlan For Success Journal™

LFWP LifePlan For Success Journal™

LFWP LifePlan For Success Journal™

LFWP LifePlan For Success Journal™

LFWP LifePlan For Success Journal™

LFWP LifePlan For Success Journal™

LFWP LifePlan For Success Journal™

LFWP LifePlan For Success Journal™

LFWP LifePlan For Success Journal™

LFWP LifePlan For Success Journal™

LFWP LifePlan For Success Journal™

LFWP LifePlan For Success Journal™

LFWP LifePlan For Success Journal™

LFWP LifePlan For Success Journal™

As a mastermind and visionary in the industry of Network Distribution, a dynamic speaker, self-improvement coach, cutting-edge entrepreneur and phenomenal author, C. Anthony Harris has successfully trained and empowered over 35,000 individuals across the United States and abroad with a way of life that demands success.

Committed to developing a movement of successful, positive, and progressive leaders, Harris is literally changing the quality of the lives he touches-spiritually, mentally, physically, professionally and financially. Through his Living the Five Wealth Principles book, CD series and personal training sessions, individuals are taught to understand the importance of and effectively apply the principles of Persistency, Consistency, Discipline, Urgency and Excitement in everything they do while reaching their highest personal and professional potential.

His philosophy that "life works when you work it" is the motivating force behind the LFWP LifePlan for Success, a tool that helps individuals not only put into perspective where they are in life and where they desire to be, but also teaches them how to develop a "LifePlan" to get there. "Success", he says, "is not just a measure of achievement, but a unique lifestyle that should be enjoyed by all."

Understanding the importance of developing an LFWP lifestyle early, Harris travels the country speaking with and training teens in the areas of entrepreneurship and leadership. Fifty percent of designated proceeds from the LFWP movement are contributed to life-improvement education programs in inner-city schools throughout the United States.